INSIGNIFICANCE
THE BOOK

First published in Great Britain in 1985
by **Sidgwick and Jackson Limited**

Copyright © 1985 by **Zenith Productions**

Designed by **Jon Barraclough**
Written by **Neil Norman** with **Penny Cherns**

ISBN 0-283-99218-2

Typeset by Land & Unwin (Data Sciences) Ltd., Bugbrooke, Northants.
Printed in Great Britain by
R.J. Acford, Industrial Estate, Chichester, West Sussex
for Sidgwick and Jackson Limited
1 Tavistock Chambers, Bloomsbury Way
London. WC1A 2SG

INSIGNIFICANCE
THE BOOK

NEIL NORMAN
AND
JON BARRACLOUGH

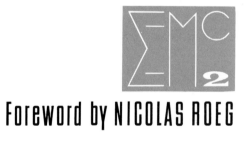

Foreword by NICOLAS ROEG

SIDGWICK & JACKSON
LONDON

FOREWORD

This is not an introduction to this book, nor do I think it is an introduction to my film of Terry Johnson's play called *Insignificance*. But then the film is not an introduction to the play, nor vice versa, but all are linked, as everything is – entertainment, science, fun, art, crime and politics. All knowledge is connected.

A couple of years ago Alexander Stuart asked me if I'd like to see a play at the Royal Court Theatre that he thought might make an interesting film. Well, I am not a great theatregoer and I don't like to take my entertainments or my life with an ever-alert eye on what might be an opportunity to twist or turn into a film. It seems to be my lot to be in the tradition of those who stumble along until a connection is made. I've never been very lucky with forced meetings or well set-up 'blind dates'. Is it a coincidence, as I look at my bookshelves, that I see *The Probability of the Impossible*, *The Challenge of Chance*, *The Roots of Coincidence*?

A couple of weeks after that first call I spoke to Alex again. He said the play was coming off at the end of the week and he had two tickets; if I could make it, he'd let me have them. I was on my own that week; my friend and producer, Jeremy Thomas, was away and his wife Eski was alone too.... So we went to the theatre and had a very jolly evening and enjoyed the play. No connections were made.

Days and weeks go by in life and my thoughts of love, life, hopes and dreams flip about in such a random way that it seems they have no pattern at all, until it gets to the point when I feel that I must find some order, and then in a half-conscious way I look for some common root or at least a staging-post or milestone from which to get my bearings.

In this case, at that moment I thought of the play and the people who inhabited it. I don't know what order Terry Johnson's thoughts had made of things in order to write his play, but somewhere his connections had linked with mine. More than likely from different routes and for different reasons, but they were forming a chain with mine and I wanted to take his play and make a film of it.

To me the characters were mythic, not invented by any single person, not the public or the press, probably not even by the characters themselves. Familiar but strange, living or dead people made up from stories, fictions, gossip. Truly fictional people, but their fiction was made up of so many other fictions that they could represent something to everyone. Here reality had reversed itself with fictions and fictions with reality. Everything seemed suddenly connected. The chain seemed endless and when the film began to take shape even the actors themselves seemed part of this endless linking.

Something was stumbled upon, something was true. When we were shooting in New York a member of the crew thought he had heard somewhere that in fact something very close to the story had indeed happened; I think he would have liked it to have – in the perfect chain reaction it probably would have. Maybe it did. I'm glad you bought the book. I hope you see the film and I hope you make a connection with a little bit of you in one of those shadows flickering on the screen.

Nicolas Roeg
1985

CONTENTS

1

THE MAKING OF MYTH

'...you can't stop or you'll be lost so you go ahead, even though you don't know where you're going, because you never know. You just have to leave from where you've been.' (William de Kooning, *New York Sunday Times*, December 1983)

Perhaps towards the end of life we can say, as Einstein did, 'The strange thing about growing old is that intimate identification with here and now is slowly lost; one feels transposed into infinity, more or less alone, no longer in hope or fear, only observing.'

Shared perceptions help us to understand each other, our world and to cope with the unknown. But how are these mythical figures selected? What makes certain tales or people the stuff of myth? Can we trace a continuous pattern or need?

A legend like that of Robin Hood, who was 'feared by the bad, loved by the good', helps reinforce morality, but the myth of King Arthur and his Knights elevates our history to a sense of Destiny and links sexual misbehaviour and betrayal to the collapse of order, thus elevating certain forms of behaviour to the plane of the supernatural and lending significance to ideals of patriotism, brotherhood, crusading zeal, etc. A myth can grow and develop over the centuries, the traditional components becoming reorganized in the light of new circumstances. Thus the Arthurian ideal becomes the image of the Kennedy period of White House rule; the story of Camelot becomes a heart-rending tale of the sexual triangle. 'Certain stories seem to have a peculiar significance: they are the stories that tell a society what it is important for them to know' (Northrop-Frye, *The Great Code*).

At certain stages new myths and rituals are created and the past is dramatized to make the future destiny apparent.
'In the hour of danger, life throws off all inessen-tials, all excrescences, all its adipose tissue, and tries to strip itself, to reduce itself to pure nerve, pure muscle. Life'is, in itself and forever, shipwreck. To be shipwrecked is not to drown. The poor human being, feeling himself sinking into the abyss, moves his arms to keep afloat. This movement of the arms which is his reaction against his own destruction, is culture – a swimming stroke. When culture is no more than this, it fulfils its function and the human being rises above his own abyss. But ten centuries of cultural continuity brings with it – among many advantages – the great disadvantage that man believes himself safe, loses the feeling of shipwreck, and his culture proceeds to burden itself with parasitic and lymphatic matter. Some discontinuity must therefore intervene, in order that man may renew his feeling of peril. All his life-saving equipment must fail, he must find nothing to cling to. Then his arms will once again move redeemingly. Consciousness of shipwreck being the truth of life constitutes salvation.' (Ortega y Gasset, *The Dehumanization of Art*).

We need some explanation of how the present condition is an episode and a significant one in an ongoing drama; in the midst of chaos someone is needed to posit a theory of unity. Albert Einstein – a man of far from superhuman qualities, not a major success at school – appeared at a time of upheaval with a unifying theory. 'Now but only now, we know that the forces which move electrons in their ellipses about the nuclei of atoms is the same force which moves our earth in its annual course about the sun, and is the same force which brings to us the rays of heat and life which make

Reinforcing morality with a longbow. (Richard Greene)
I.T.C. Entertainment Limited

'An extraordinarily satisfactory human being.'

Making the myth fit. At 44, Monty stopped growing and died.

life possible upon this planet,' (1929 interview) and yet ironically and with true nemesis he was to be responsible for unleashing upon the world the most destructive forces of all – within that very order is chaos.

Einstein was turned into a symbol throughout the world – a symbol of achievement – but also someone who had challenged the chaos in the cosmos – found an external authorization. As he said himself, commenting on his early loss of a belief in a god who dealt with human affairs, 'To punish me for my contempt for authority, Fate made me an authority myself.' He also knew that implied in the impossibility of such a high achievement was a resounding rejection, 'If relativity is proved right the Germans will call me a German, the Swiss will call me a Swiss citizen, and the French will call me a great scientist. If relativity is proved wrong the French will call me a Swiss, the Swiss will call me a German and the Germans will call me a Jew.'

PROFESSOR In my lifetime I have been accused by the Swiss of being a German Fascist, by the Germans of being a Zionist Conspirator, and by the Americans of being a German Fascist, a Zionist Conspirator, and now a Soviet Communist. By two magazines in one week I was called a conscientious objector and a warmonger. Both magazines were reviewing a speech I made to the Mozart Appreciation Society of New England. Now you want to know if I deserve to be called an American.

He had located the huge energy residing in a mass ...and now, for all of us, the abdication of responsibility for understanding science and technology means that one accepts subordination to the power of the technocrats. It allows the continuation of the ancient priest class as a repository of secret and therefore powerful knowledge. This was the role awarded to Einstein – a myth himself and a keeper of myths. He suffered the veneration and the rejection classically shown to the genius who like the madman is sometimes wooed and sometimes shunned.

We clothe the individual's achievement in the garments of transcendence over the mass society and then demand as reward our right to debunk them...the current trend for documentary dramas is to remove the well-known lines shimmering with a sense of destiny and give the heroes instead a mundane and 'normal' dialogue.

Marilyn was a perfect subject for mythologizing – coming from nowhere, in fact from near-orphan circumstances – reared in a loveless childhood she became a love/sex goddess through her own achievement, not through superhuman qualities...it could happen to anyone.... Like Aphrodite (or Eve) she was permanently offering the apple of temptation to the prince/king/man who would temporarily be allowed to enter the orchard of paradise and rule with her for a while.

Marilyn was 'soft' and 'vulnerable' and therefore could be tamed and dominated by far from macho men figures (witness some of her co-stars). Marilyn was melted by the heat. All mythologies are explanations of the unknown by reference to extrapolations of the known. Marilyn had something that seemed an inexplicable and rather magical quality; the answer was to try and strip it down, probe and pummel it until it was naked and unadorned. In Magic you only need an object belonging to the person to bewitch them; Pythagoreans used to obey the injunction to smooth the bed soon after rising to remove the imprint of the body so that it could not be used to the owner's detriment; in popular romance or pop songs, a kiss would be treasured and the area kissed left unwashed ('Your sweet red lips just kissed my cheek and I aint a goin' to wash for a week' – Brooks Brothers, 1962).

Montgomery Clift said, 'If you have a goal – and are busy growing – you're safe. It's only when you believe of yourself what the general public believes that you start losing the courage to risk outward failure. That is the biggest pitfall. Look out!' (Clift, letter to Ned Smith, quoted *Short Lives*.) He died at the age of forty-four.

As with Marilyn Monroe, the ending gave a beginning and a middle and therefore turned their lives into works of art with a message, a meaning; or perhaps solidified the image that first gave them their mythical status – forever entering the underworld of the inexplicable forces that frighten and puzzle us. We create our adventure, our sense of living dangerously, through other people, others' legends. How far is the scapegoat from the hero?

Perhaps an even greater example of fetishism of objects is given by the collecting of cards carrying the portraits of sports heroes. The first World Series was played in 1903 with the National and the American League. Popular excitement with the game grew after Babe Ruth (with an orphaned

Bubblegum myths. Baseball heroes elevated to the status of icons were reduced to bubblegum card cartoons. The untouchable becomes the collectable. Four U.S. sports heroes achieve immortality through caricature. © *1985 Paul Cemmick*

Three strikes and you're out. 'You play ball with me and . . .'

background which already removed him from the mundanity of normal human parentage – a good start for heroic and mythological status) hit 29 home runs for the Boston Red Sox in 1919. A new home game was invented. Babe Ruth was succeeded in the baseball Olympiad by Joe Di Maggio. 'He was the perfect player: he possessed in his quiet way the same on-field as well as off-field magic that Babe Ruth did, mesmerising the public with his undemonstrative personality as surely as Ruth had with his totally uninhibited ways.' The Cincinnati Red Stockings, the first professional baseball team, had toured the nation and remained undefeated after fifty-six contests. Di Maggio hit home safely in fifty-six consecutive games. In baseball, fifty-six became a magic number.

In early nineteenth-century America, where baseball was nursed, the country was a half tamed wilderness – a perfect setting for the heroic age. Whereas in Europe heroes had moved through oral legend to written literature over a period of time

which enabled the myth to be purified and filtered, in America the man and the oral tradition, closely followed by written 'autobiographies', co-existed. The distance was provided by space and mediated by territorial boundaries rather than by time. Davy Crockett (King of the Wild Frontier), who 'Killed him a bear when he was only three', like Hercules was not written down in any American counterpart of the *Morte d'Arthur*. Crockett anecdotes plunged headlong in a decade from the small world of fireside stories and bar room wheeze into the great democratic world of print.... They entered at once into a thriving subliterature.

'Readers of the Crockett legends are never quite certain whether to laugh or applaud.' Even today when we are looking back at the heroes of that age we may wonder, as Boorstin did, 'Are we admiring the beautiful, the grand, the big or the ugly?' Sergio Leone captures this beautifully in his retelling of the history of the American West, even capturing the idea of (this time) *The Good, The Bad and The*

Ugly. The Cowboy Legend – one of the first and main staples of the early cinema – carries within it the whole ambiguity of the American hero. In a film like *One Eyed Jacks*, for instance, a two-bit no good semi-gangster is made an ambiguous kind of glamorous figure by the very fact of being singled out for presentation; on top of which he is played by a beautiful actor (Brando) and is seen in the cinema larger than life – the size of an icon. But this is all part of the American hunt for its history.

As scientific enquiry proceeds, mankind gets better at inventing things that are more and more dangerous. In America, a nation where to be first was all – to be there first and fast was more important than serving the future – the notion of built-in obsolescence gained ground; it has to be newer, more spontaneous, bigger, better, held up for all to see, franchised, marketed as widely as possible and then replaced. This has been true of artefacts and, as we have seen, of people. What could be bigger and brighter than a star, and what could burn out quicker? The most recent offering was a genuine hurtling towards the sun ... a process chronicled by Tom Wolfe in *The Right Stuff*, the story of the first astronauts. This is the story of who has the Right Stuff and who is left behind.

'Never again would an astronaut be perceived as a protector of the people, risking his life to do battle in the heavens.... The Lord giveth and the Lord taketh away. The mantle of Cold Warrior of the Heavens had been placed on their shoulders one April day in 1959 without their asking for it or having anything to do with it or even knowing it. And now it would be taken away, without their knowing that either and because of nothing they ever did or desired.'

They had been used, fed back with mythological status so that the country could see themselves in the astronauts and the astronauts in themselves, and the destiny of the nation being acted out in its race into space against communist Russia. And now they were dropped.

The Senator checks up on potential subversives.

Joe McCarthy's lauding sprang from the Founding Fathers; it had its roots in the gargantuan terrible/overblown epics of Davy Crockett.

But there is no simple line: 'The sad truth is that man's real life consists of a complex of inexorable opposites: day and night, birth and death, happiness and misery, good and evil. We are not even sure that one will prevail against the other, that good will overcome evil or joy defeat pain. Life is a battle ground. It always has been, and always will be; and if it were not so, existence would come to an end.' (Jung, *Approaching the Unconscious*.) We have the choice between seemingly irreconcilable oppositions. In our drive to control the social environment and to place ourselves within it and give it and us context and significance, we use devices that simplify a complex reality and enable our belief systems to remain intact and validated as the contradictions of our world.

'And late at night, as the white fire coals deepen into black, we tell of our great souls. Silent were their footsteps through the pine forests, across the buffalo grass, and into the canyons. And when their footsteps brought them to that chasm beyond which men venture once only, they vanished from our midst. Likely it is we shall not see their equal again. But as they left their work and spirit forever with us their people, so even as they journey on they leave an imperishable mark upon the sky, for there, arching across the heavens, is the pathway of souls. We do not know where their journey leads.

Nor do we know what sights they may behold. And in the night each bright star is a campfire blazing in the sky where they have paused in their journey to look down on us their people, as we huddle for warmth around the campfire.' (Adapted from an Algonquin myth by Olcott.)

We may be far from identifying mining with tearing open our mothers but the longing to be a part of things is still with us.

Still we hunt for ways across the abyss – still we look for saviours, rebirth, the pure hero/heroine who achieves through personal struggle, who will save us, die for us, challenge the powers of darkness, the wild beasts. Yet for those to whom we look to give us a sense of meaning, of our own significance, we reserve the right to render them insignificant and thereby preserve ourselves in the image of gods. The mythological structure is intact.

There's nothing then to pray for? If you pray,
pray for the gods and Jupiter to help.
What's best, what serves us, only He can know.
We're dearer to the gods than to ourselves.
Hurried by impulse and by diseased desire.
We ask for wives, and children by our wives –
what wives, what children, heaven only knows.
Still, if you ask for something, if you must
buy holy sausages and dedicate
the tripe of bulls at every altar, pray for
a healthy body and a healthy soul,
a soul that is not terrified by death,
that thinks long life the least of nature's gifts,
courage that takes whatever comes – this hero
like Hercules, all pain and labour, loathes
the lecherous gut of Sardanapalus.
Success is worshipped as a god; it's we
who set up shrines and temples in her name.
I give you simply what you have already.
(Lowell, 'The Vanity of Human Wishes'; a
version of Juvenal's Tenth Satire.)

Travel by subway and see The Promised Land.

TE. 035

2

SCOUNDREL TIME

The term 'Scoundreltime' was coined by the writer Lillian Hellman,[1] one of many artists whose testimony was demanded by the House Committee on Un-American Activities (HUAC). The time's most enthusiastic scoundrel was Senator Joe McCarthy, a man who sought the same relationship with communists that Buffalo Bill had achieved with the North American bison. McCarthy is the symbol of the infamous and hysterical Red-baiting of the era; he did not create the fishing fleet. He was simply the masthead on the Cold War's ship of fools.

President Truman had a political enemy at home – the first Republican Congress in sixteen years – and had found a new threat abroad: the spectre of international communism. His political strategy in devising what became known as the Cold War may have confused the mass of Americans who had happily assimilated the information that the Russians were America's brave allies. With the threat of fascism seemingly abolished, a new enemy was created: Reds hungry for the souls of innocent Americans, vampires of the democratic impulse.

Such was the Reds' subversive power, it was thought, that they had already infiltrated American society and their dupes must be sought out and effectively dealt with. Accordingly, in the spring of 1947 Truman's Attorney General compiled a list of organizations: communist, fascist, totalitarian and subversive. No member of these groups could be approved for a job in the federal services without thorough investigation. The pertinent question, of course: are you now or have you ever been ...?

In total violation of US civil rights the list was then published and the witch hunters, freed from the constraints of the constitution, were set upon the nation. Somehow the notion that these checks were necessary for federal employees developed into a much wider and more dangerous idea: these checks were necessary to be American. As the very ethos of the nation was being eroded, no holds were barred in seeking out the Reds: neighbours and workmates were encouraged to brand their colleagues. Even writers and film-makers who had

'Are you now or have you ever been . . . ?'

The Senator auditions for Slander, Inc.

praised the Russian Allies in years past were now required to justify their 'communist sympathies'. The Attorney General's list had not simply unleashed the dogs of war but also the hyenas of prejudice, persecution and cankerous envy.

The dual investigations produced a confused melodrama of villains, heroes and victims, and many who simply found themselves lacking in courage. Some spoke, some broke, some never worked in their chosen professions again. HUAC or McCarthy sought them all: Alger Hiss, Paul Robeson, Elia Kazan, Sterling Hayden, Bertolt Brecht, Albert Einstein, Arthur Miller. And the Hollywood Ten.

The Hollywood Ten is remembered as a *cause célèbre*; the Hollywood ten aren't. Indicted for contempt and sent to jail because of their refusal to testify as the Committee wished, they saw their careers collapse or go into a seemingly endless limbo. They were mostly writers rather than stars, their names largely unknown, though their films had been seen by millions. Many of their names had been on a list compiled by AWARE, a self-appointed vigilante group. One of them, the film

director Edward Dymytryk, changed his mind, came out of jail and became a star witness for the Committee. In 1956 the writer Robert Rich won the Academy Award for best screenplay for *The Brave One*. He wasn't there to accept Hollywood's highest accolade. Many were embarrassed later when it was disclosed that Robert Rich did not in fact exist: Rich was Dalton Trumbo, one of the Ten, and a man who had been told he'd never work in Hollywood again. Are you now or have you ever been?

> SENATOR Seems to me there's only yes or no, but there are some citizens don't like to use either of them words .... You know the most times one man has cited the Fifth Amendment? Seventy-nine times. He got awful tired ... we had to spend two extra sessions trying that jumped up nigger Robeson for contempt ....

As McCarthy and his fellow senators delved ever deeper into the shallows of Hollywood, some citizens saw the danger. Harold Taylor, President

A political cover-up. The Senator discovers that his credibility is receding.

Hot words in The Cold War. McCarthy brutalizes a witness during his investigation of subversives in the Army in 1953. Special Army Counsel Joseph Welch, appalled at McCarthy's bullyboy tactics, eventually lost his composure and exclaimed: 'Let us not assassinate this lad further, Senator. You have done enough. Have you no sense of decency, sir, at long last? Have you left no sense of decency?'

of Sarah Lawrence College, provided a considered definition of HUAC's ideal patriotic American:

One who tells all his secrets without being asked, believes we should go to war with Russia, holds no political view without prior consultation with his employer, does not ask for increases in wages or salary and is in favor of peace, universal military training, brotherhood and baseball. [2]

Baseball, at least, was all-American.

'I killed more people tonight than I have fingers on my hands. I shot them in cold blood and enjoyed every minute of it .... They were Commies, Lee. Red sons of bitches who should have died long ago .... They never thought that there were people like me in this country. They figured us all to be soft as horse manure and just as stupid.'

That was the voice, from Mickey Spillane's *One Lonely Night*, of Mike Hammer, private eye, self-appointed political and moral vigilante and the kind of good citizen who would have memorized the lists published by AWARE. He was an emblem of male attitudes in sex and the nation's attitude in politics. Spillane was the keeper of the national paranoia, the voice of a nation deep in the throes of political terror – and presented the brutal, sexy hero of every twelve-year-old kid reading illicitly by torchlight under the bedclothes. Unlike Joe McCarthy, Mike Hammer didn't ask questions first.

As HUAC sought the canker in the nation's culture, so popular culture responded by redefining the world. Even geographical bubble-gum cards which included information about a country called the USSR – 'population 211,000,000' – were banned. The biggest country in the world disappeared overnight so that the children of America could sleep safely. No matter.

In a world where art, or indeed popular culture, is treated with suspicion, the real enemy is the intellectual. In America in the 1950s, to men like McCarthy intellectuals were foreign, foreign was elsewhere than America, elsewhere than America was by definition Russia and thus, clearly, intellec-

tuals were Russians or Russian dupes. The melting pot that had made America was consigned to the back burner and the intellectuals caught the full heat, squirming on the griddle. The Hollywood that existed was a mythical land, in part built on the dreams of émigrés, which was what made it such a dangerous place. Brecht and Albert Einstein were foreign and, God knows, intellectuals and therefore prime targets for subpoena. But intellectuals are produced by education and therefore educationalists also came under suspicion.

William Frauenglass, a Brooklyn teacher, was called before the Committee. He fully understood the nature of the attack. Knowing that Albert Einstein had discreetly condemned the inquisitors, Frauenglass sought to encourage the scientist to a stronger and more public statement. Einstein responded to the case in a letter to the *New York Times*:

The problem with which the intellectuals of this country are confronted is very serious. Reactionary politicians have managed to instil suspicion of all intellectual efforts into the public by dangling before their eyes a danger from without. Having succeeded so far, they are now proceeding to suppress the freedom of teaching and to deprive of their positions all those who do not prove submissive, i.e. to starve them out.

What ought the minority of intellectuals to do against the evil? Frankly, I can only see the revolutionary way of non-cooperation in the sense of Gandhi. Every intellectual who is called before one of the committees ought to refuse to testify, i.e. he must be prepared for jail and economic ruin, in short, for the sacrifice of his personal welfare in the interest of the cultural welfare of his country .... If enough people are ready to take this grave step they will be successful. If not, then the intellectuals of this country deserve nothing better than the slavery which is intended for them.

When Einstein added a postscript, 'this letter need not be considered confidential', the result became inevitable. The letter caused a sensation and Einstein was placed in the forefront of the arguments

In the hands of the truly great, art and science are inseparable. Music can move masses as effectively as the bomb. While Hitler sought inspiration from Wagner, Einstein played Mozart between calculations.

The Professor's fishing expedition is discouraged by Nazi youths.

about freedom and intellectual liberty.

Red-baiting had acquired an opponent of stature: a man of compassion, insight and commitment, a scientist and an international icon.

Einstein was an extraordinarily satisfactory human being. In spite of his genius and his fame, he always behaved with complete simplicity and never seemed to be claiming any superiority.

Einstein, throughout his life, cared for the individual and for individual liberty. He showed, himself, all the courage that his circumstances demanded and called upon others, often without success, to show equal courage. He had seen individual freedom lost in Germany with the advent of the Nazis, and he was quickly perceptive of any danger of a like disaster in other countries. He had small respect for the Big Battalions, and his attitude to governments was very like that of the Hebrew prophets. He was not only a great scientist but a great man.[4]

Thus wrote Bertrand Russell in a preface to *Einstein on Peace* by Otto Nathan and Heinz Norden.

As Einstein called for civil disobedience and a refusal to comply with the illegal interrogations of the baying senator, the mood of the country had already begun to change. The Archbishop of Washington warned of politicians who preferred to 'seize upon any issue, real or spurious, to boost their fame and publicity'. Senator Symington of Missouri warned of a 'new reign of terror'. Support for Red-hunting began to dwindle and McCarthy looked more and more like a man not in full possession of his senses. As the country was slowly inoculated with good sense, the disease in McCarthy's hysteria became ever more evident.

Hubris destroyed the senator's schemes. As he turned his attentions from the arts to the army he discovered that there were vested interests greater than the fear of communism and territorial imperatives within America's own shores. The government became disquieted at the prospect of his inquisition delving into and dividing the nation's defence. Mostly people didn't want to know any

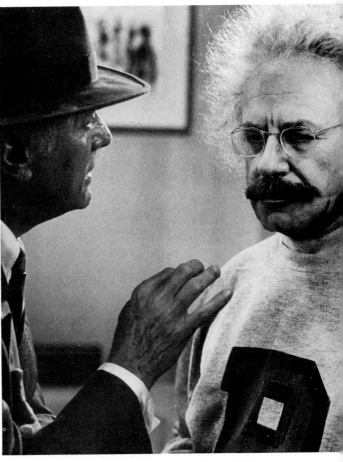

The Senator threatens The Professor with a small but effective mud pie.

more. The congressional committees – self-designated as 'Grand Juries' – operated in public. The accusations they threw stuck to the 'witnesses' whether there was any truth in them or not. And more and more the frenzied questioning looked desperate. Supporters and detractors alike called it all 'a fishing expedition'.

> SENATOR I'd put you in the same category as some of the movie people we've talked to; the type of person to whom mud sticks.

> PROFESSOR I am here to speak at the conference for world peace. The date of my subpoena coincides quite beautifully but it will not prevent me from attending. Nor if I had arranged to go fishing would it have prevented me from catching fish.

Mr and Mrs Einstein getting away from it all.

Genius with pipe and piano.

Miller and Monroe: Beauty and the Brain. Marriage to Marilyn got the playwright off the hook and a new passport to boot.

Private tragedy descended into public farce. Arthur Miller appeared before HUAC in 1956 in a race to get a passport, and *Time* magazine reported in a way that suggested the nation's attention was drifting far from the madding crowd:

No, he had never been under Communist Party discipline. Yes, he had indeed lent his name and support to many a Red-front group in the 1940s. No, he was no longer in 'the mood' to support 'a cause dominated by Communists'. At only one hurdle did Pulitzer prizewinner Miller balk. He would not provide the names of his former Red associates. 'I will tell you anything about myself,' said he frankly, 'but I cannot take responsibility for another human being.' At hearing's end, it looked as if Miller would get 1) his passport, 2) a contempt citation for clamming about his old friends. But he soon reduced the hearing to a subplot and grabbed the headlines by unclamming about a newer friend. To newsmen, Miller confided that he needed a passport by 13 July, the day that Cinemactress Marilyn Monroe flies to London to begin work on The Sleeping Prince *with Sir Laurence Olivier. Reason: 'She will go as Mrs Miller.' Later in Manhattan the lovebirds billed and cooed for lensmen outside Marilyn's apartment house.*

PROFESSOR Because of being famous, everywhere I go people fall over themselves to be with me, like a troupe of clowns chasing an old automobile. Because of fame, everything I do develops into a ridiculous comedy.

Fame got you on to the hook and finally fame got you off the hook. The famous had the last laugh though it left a bitter taste in the mouth. In the international eye, as America's most significant playwright, now the fiancé of American's most famous blonde, Arthur Miller survived the fishing expedition and was issued his passport.

The publicity McCarthy had sought consumed him. Senator Lyndon Johnson, Senate minority leader, worked to pass the motion of censure that brought with it the destruction of McCarthy's powerbase. Ed Murrow and the power of televison hammered nails in the coffin.

**Mrs Miller succumbs to the overdressed charms of
Olivier's Prince.**

Familiarity breeds contempt.
Within four years, McCarthyism
had changed from a household
word to an obscenity. © 1985 Paul
Cemmick

It seems unlikely that McCarthy ever sought the help of a psychiatrist, though several members of that profession clearly took pleasure in observing him. Those who wrote on the subject stressed the elements of classical paranoia; delusions of persecution; delusions of grandeur. In 1954 one anonymous author noted:

The significant thing about McCarthy is the extraordinary intensity of his neurotic drives. The key to understanding is the recognition of his basic insecurity, self-doubt and self-contempt.

McCarthy's mental health remains a matter for speculation. His physical health was clearly poor, to say the least. The censure vote was delayed until mid-1955 because of McCarthy's hospitalization with what was described as 'traumatic bursitis'. Like most of his wilder accusations, McCarthy's own ailments remain unsubstantiated: back trouble, leg trouble, liver trouble, prostate trouble, lung trouble, heart trouble, herniated-diaphragm trouble and, always, alcohol trouble.

He was a heavy drinker, one whose idea of going on the wagon was substituting beer for bourbon. His dentist allowed him to rinse his mouth out with whisky, and even at the congressional hearings he had frequent recourse to a bottle of cough medicine in a brown paper bag. Finally, as an ex-marine, he was admitted to a Naval Medical Centre where peripheral neuritis (an inflammation of the nerve ends associated with alcoholism) was diagnosed.

He died on 2 May 1957 at 6 p.m. 'Just in time,' noted one of his associates,' 'for the seven o'clock news.' His years of publicity and humiliation had all come full circle. Any native American might have noted that this was indeed the nature of the world.

Scoundreltime was at its end; its legacy may never disappear. When demons are summoned they do not depart with grace. McCarthy was the first lesson of the Atomic Age.

The second lesson was the Bomb and How to Live with It.

Inquisitor at bay. McCarthy begins
to lose his grip. Scoundreltime
draws to a close.

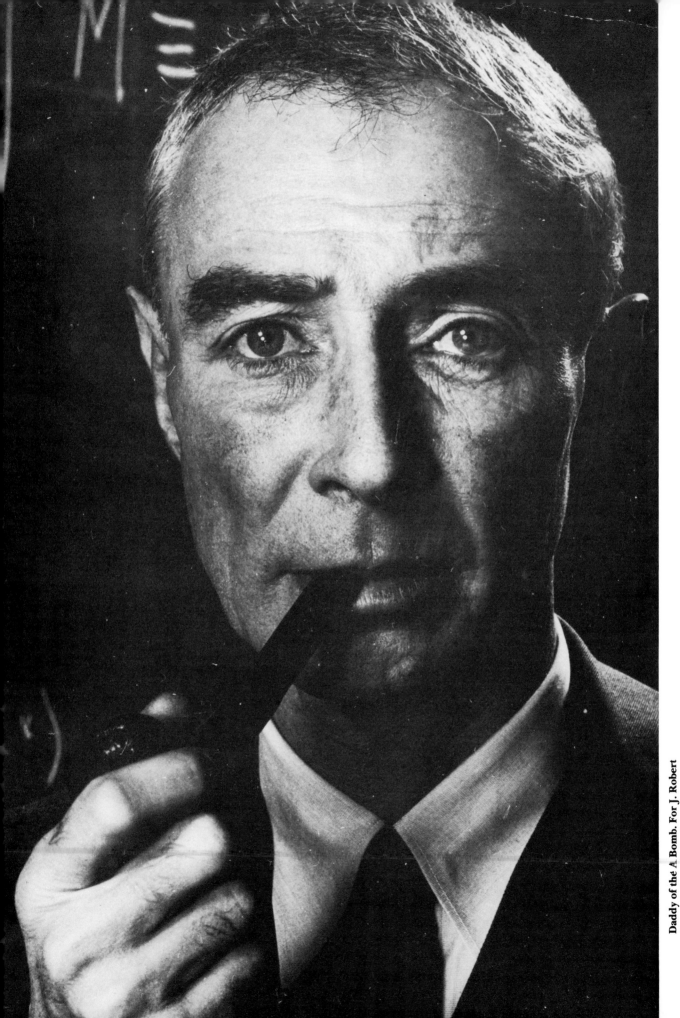

Daddy of the A Bomb. For J. Robert Oppenheimer, fatherhood became an intolerable burden.

The fifties were the Atomic Age and the bomb had changed everything. When the Soviet Union developed its own, the Cold War opened the doors for a game of thermonuclear chess. HUAC provided protection from the commies inside, but that gave no answers to what you might do about the Ruskies flying above your head. The Council on Atomic Implications, not in the slightest perplexed by its own name, issued the pamphlet 'Atomic Attack, a Manual for Survival', and *Time* ran a sardonic appraisal:

Time was when a small American who got vaccinated and looked both ways before crossing streets had a reasonable chance of outliving his boyhood. But a new complication to survival has been added. One recent treatise on the subject seriously inquired: 'Can Junior fall instantly face down, elbow out, forehead on elbow, eyes shut? Have him try it tonight as he gets out of bed.'

Junior could probably master the trick – practice and understanding might after all save the life of a small boy born into the Atomic Age.

Junior will feel the wind go by, the dirt and pebbles blown with hurricane force against his head ....

A few cuts on the arms and legs aren't important. His playmates, standing upright, will be blown over like matchsticks. Some may get concussion, some broken bones.

Ludicrous advice, but no more so than the wisdom contained in a bouncy little number called 'Duck and Cover', a song in which this is indeed the main message: if there's a nuclear bomb dropped near you, duck and cover. But then hard information was scarce, even when it was fully understood by those in the know. It's clear now that not even the Council on Atomic Implications could have known *all* the implications.

The threat of a commie bomb remained. They intended to wipe out not only you but your children and their children. An American bomb represented peace – after all, it had brought peace – but a Russian bomb could be quite different .... When the bomb became a threat rather than a treasured possession, new approaches became necessary. And, as is to be expected, they came from the unlikeliest sources.

In 1953 President Dwight D. Eisenhower proposed at the UN General Assembly that America, the Soviet Union and Britain donated isotopes to a common fund for peaceful purposes: a Holy Grail of solid radiation. In his memoirs[5] he remembered the proposal:

My objectives in this talk were several. The principal one was exactly as stated – to make a clear effort to get the Soviet Union working with us in a noncontroversial phase of the atomic field and thus begin to divert nuclear science from destructive to peaceful purposes.

HUAC, 1948. All men are corruptible, but some are more corruptible than others. The godfather of the HUAC, J. Parnell Thomas, *right,* **was indicted for padding his congressional payroll. The ambitious lawyer,** *left,* **eventually achieved infamy of a more celebrated kind.**

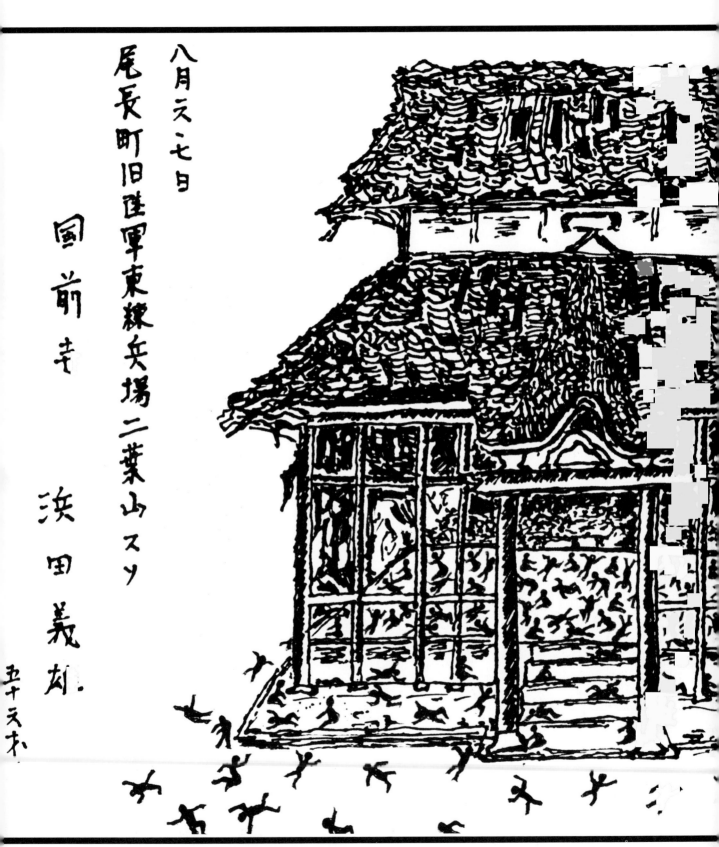

ACTRESS: '. . . Unless of course they could blow up all the
people and leave the buildings standing, which they can't.'
From *The Unforgettable Fire* pictures drawn by survivors of the
atomic bomb, Hiroshima 1945.

The second was that if we were successful in making even a start, it was possible that gradually negotiation and cooperation might expand into something broader; there was hope that Russia's self-interest might lead her to participate in joint humanitarian efforts.

A third objective was to call the attention of smaller nations to the fact that they too had an interest in the uses to which the world put its limited supply of fissionable material. Too many small nations had looked upon nuclear science as a matter of concern only to the USSR and the United States, except, of course, for the fear that their own countries might be targets in the event of atomic war.

My hope was to awaken in these nations an understanding that new and promising opportunities were steadily opening up for using these materials and skills for their benefit. Thus world opinion might build for turning efforts towards these constructive purposes.

Now that the Russians had the bomb it had been inadvertently revealed as a weapon of aggression, and its only users should turn it into a tool of peace. McCarthy asked innocent questions; America made innocent bombs. Eisenhower would reassure Americans that they had not supported nuclear development only to see it used as a means of world destruction. It was a bomb to build on, a demonstration of America's capabilities – not a story of truculence, defiance and threat.

The press gave the speech its title: 'Atoms for Peace'.

As Eisenhower's benign paternal gaze encompassed the nation, reassuring Americans that the commies were on the run, memories of Hiroshima were fading into a new era – an era of economic and cultural expansion.

A new race was born in America. They were called teenagers. And the world was theirs.

What are you rebelling against?
What've you got?
Marlon Brando in *The Wild One*, 1954.

The original rebel – with more causes than most.

Spotlighting **JAMES DEAN** star, answers some personal questions for Film Show Annual readers — Warner Bros. new sensational

JAMES DEAN is my real name. . . . Height? 5 feet 10 inches . . . Weight? 155 pounds . . . Colour of eyes? Blue . . . Hair? Blond . . . Nationality? American . . . Where were you born? Fairmount, Indiana . . . Date of Birth? February 8, 1931. . . . What schools did you attend? Grammar and High School in Fairmount. College? University of California at Los Angeles. In what school sports did you participate? Baseball, track, basketball. Did you take part in school dramatics? Yes. Were any of your relatives theatrical people? No. Who brought you up? My uncle and aunt, as my mother died while I was a baby. When did you start acting? In High School. To whom do you give credit for stimulating your interest in acting? To James Whitmore,

who lived near the university in Los Angeles. We had many serious talks. I was taking a pre-law course then. Did you finish your course in law? No. I left the campus after two years. I decided I wanted to be a professional actor. I headed for New York. What was your first stage role? I played the role of a boy who has been shut in an ice house for ten years in "See the Jaguar". What was your next important role? The blackmailing Arab in "The Immoralist". How did you happen to go on the screen? Elia Kazan saw me in "The Immoralist" and decided to test me for East of Eden, the film he was about to produce and direct at Warner Bros. in Hollywood. List the pictures in which you have appeared? East of Eden, Rebel Without a Cause, and Giant. What arts are you most interested in outside of acting? Sailing, fencing, gymnastics, boxing, tennis, and an academic interest in bullfighting. What is your pet aversion? Nightclubs. What extravagances do you have? I buy a lot of camera equipment, buy lots of records, and keep a palomino horse. What is your taste in books? I like books that are on the serious side. I read everything from books on culture, expressionistic literature, and philosophical works. Sometimes I read six at a time, skipping from book to book—generally managing to get them all read at about the same time. Are you orderly? No—I'm told that stepping into my home in the Hollywood hills. I am not a hurricane. My belongings are strewn everywhere, in my home in the Hollywood hills. I am not always in a rush! When I don't have a call to work early on a studio set I prefer to stay up late and then try to sleep till almost noon. Unless I absolutely have to dress up off-screen, I would rather jump into old dungarees and a T-shirt. What sort of girls do you date? Usually actresses, so that we can talk more about the screen, stage and television. I don't think I am self-centred, because I am very concerned with the hopes and problems of others. In New York I sometimes took girl friends out on the rear seat of my motor-cycle. In Hollywood I have a little foreign car now and am happy to share it with my real friends.

61

There was no limit to home culture, either. For $11.50 you could paint an Old Master with a painting-by-numbers kit manufactured by the Palmer Paint Company of Detroit. TV sets were cheap and so were sunglasses and cars. Everything was new, bright, disposable, ephemeral and insignificant. There was new affluence and a new cosmetic aggression.

In 1956 outside of a newly isolationist America very little was happening:

General Nasser announced the nationalization of the Suez Canal.
Israel invaded Egypt.
The Soviet Union invaded Budapest to crush the Hungarian uprising.

Britain's first atomic power station was built at Calder Hall.
The Suez crisis erupted.
The Olympic Games were held in Melbourne, Australia. The Soviet Union won more medals than any other country.
The British Navy carried out secret nuclear tests off the coast of Australia.

In America James Dean was a *Rebel Without a Cause*. Too fast to live, too young to die and, for the young, too important to be forgotten. The commies would be dealt with, the bomb would save the world and America would lead the way.

It was the 1950s. And in the fifties, you could do anything.

Fifties' fetishes. Idolatry ran riot in the search for teenage identity. Rock 'n' Roll voodoo replaced dat ole time religion. The makers of the Presley doll claimed it did everything except sing. But what happened when Elvis' detractors stuck pins into it?

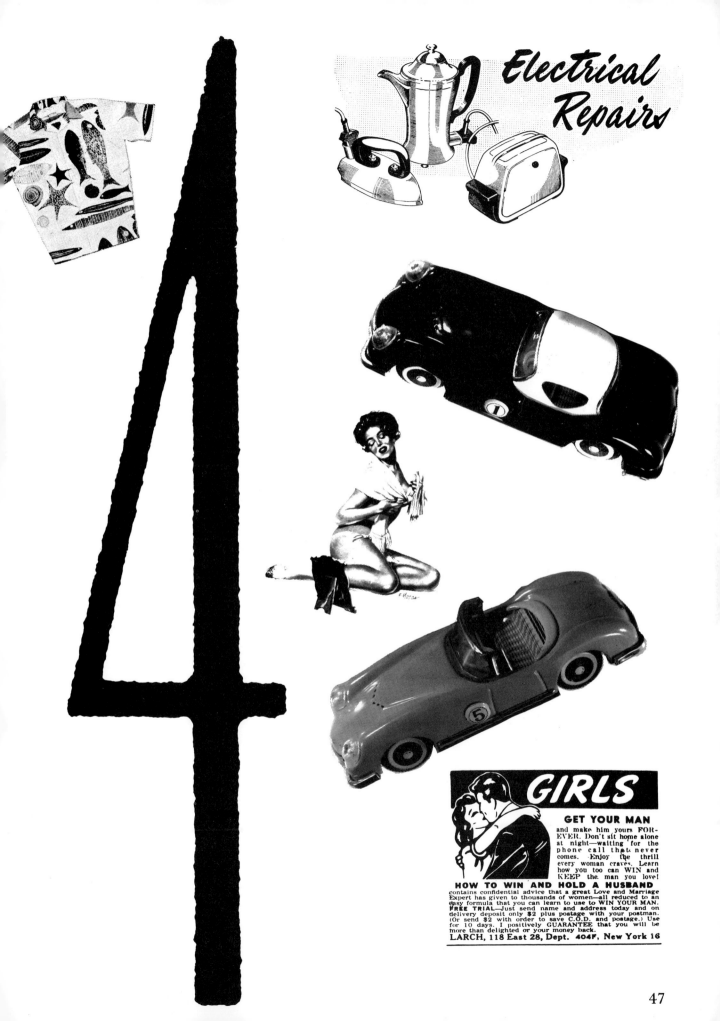

Electrical Repairs

47

Burn bright and burn out. A star goes supernova.

Images of the fifties: music, inventions, fads, fashions, cars and politics sealed in memory for one generation have been regurgitated as quasi-nostalgic factory fodder for another when invention runs dry.

The fifties saw a revolution in popular music jiving hand in hand with the hysterical beat of youth culture. Bobby-soxers had squealed their love for Sinatra, the phenomenon surrounding Presley was merely more overt in its sexuality on both sides of the footlights. What Sinatra's melting vocal tones had promised, Presley's hips seemed to deliver. The unchallenging anodyne music which was the detritus of the big band impulse, the strains of Harlem filtered into the martini glasses of Manhattan, took refuge in the hearts of account executives on Madison Avenue: the young wanted a rawer energy. What made it all even better was that their parents *hated* it.

It isn't enough to say that Elvis is kind to his parents. That still isn't a free ticket to behave like a sex maniac in public before millions of impressionable kids. According to a scholarly friend of mine, Jackie Gleason, we'll survive Elvis. He can't last, said Gleason. I tell you flatly – he can't last.

Eddie Condon, *New York Journal-American*, 1956.

On Ed Sullivan's [popular 'family-viewing' television] programme Presley injected movements of the tongue and indulged in wordless singing that were singularly distasteful. When Presley executes his bumps and grinds, it must be remembered by the Columbia Broadcasting System that even the 12-year-old's curiosity may be overstimulated.

Jack Gould, *New York Times*, 1956.

But it was too late. The teenage rebels had brought their night-time fantasies and brought them into the sunlight. Their parents had needed music to soothe away memories of war, hardship and Hiroshima. Fifties' kids were mostly more treasured than previous children. They were the living proof of survival, to be adored, pampered, given everything their parents had missed out on. No

ELVIS PELVIS

In the music business, it seems that Perry Como, with his relaxed and flaccid style of singing, makes new friends and wins new plaudits each time he makes an appearance.

On the other hand, it seems that Elvis Pelvis, with his frenzied shake, wriggle, squirm, rock and roll style of howling, makes new enemies and incites new objections each time he makes an appearance, in or out of uniform.

Since we anticipate this kind of reaction as soon as MAD makes an appearance, your Editors attended a performance of said teen-age idol in order to see what goes on.

What goes on, we observed, is Elvis's pelvis. On and on.

Candid pictures of Elvis, one-time hillbilly singer, show sensuous motions which punctuate sensuous lament. Sensuous motions and lament are caused by sentimental hangover from hillbilly days. Elvis still wears itchy red flannel underwear.

ELVIS PELVIS SINGS VARIOUS TYPES OF POP TUNES

CAREFREE CHUCKLE	HAPPY GIGGLE	HYSTERICAL HOWL

PELVIS LILTS CAREFREE CHUCKLE of the catchy "It Only Hurts When I Laugh!"

PELVIS CROONS HAPPY GIGGLE of the amusing ballad, "Electrocution Day."

PELVIS BELLOWS HYSTERICAL HOWL of revived "My Old Kentucky Home Brew."

Schmeling would have beaten Joe Louis in their second fight if the Brown Bomber hadn't got in 50 or 60 lucky punches.

4

matter that their parents wanted all-American children, tooth-capped and squeaky clean: to celebrate being alive the kids were given money. Teenagers were born out of their parents' pocketbooks. They weren't a new or a natural phenomenon, they were a new source of disposable income, the final American Dream, the newest, shiniest thing in the brand-new era: a consumer group the world had never dreamt of. And that was a powerbase so strong they could never be destroyed.

Money was circulating and culture was moving into the orbit of the masses. Communications technology, expanded by wartime research, moved ahead in leaps and bounds straight into the living rooms and dens of the nation. The speed of information and the way in which it was acquired changed: there was a nation hungry for entertainment. Radios blared, films poured out of Hollywood. Everything was *fast:* fast food, fast cars, fast culture.

Two cultures walked side by side: the horror comic and the classic novel; the Hollywood musical and *Hiroshima Mon Amour;* Norman Rockwell and Jackson Pollock.

The news-stands told their own story: a new magazine, *Playboy,* offered naked women for fifty cents. The first fold-out featured Marilyn Monroe in her legendary calendar pose with nothing on but the radio.

The new culture infiltrated the lives of patrician and proletarian alike, inexorably changed the world and its perceptions. It almost seemed, for a little while, that most of the people were pleased most of the time.

Come back to the Five and Dime, Norma Jean, Norma Jean.

THE STORY OF LIFE, DEATH, SEX AND THE UNIVERSE... RELATIVELY SPEAKING

3

1 2 **3** 4 5 6

The loneliness of the long distance actress.

Insignificance is about reality but has nothing to do with it, and it is about myth but has created its own. Here the real world and its history are not only objective 'givens' – they are also posthumous interpretations, extrapolations and completed fictions. We all, in part, film our own lives and decide who will be the bit players. We all recreate the past that we imagined, suspecting all the while that we have got it wrong. The process of doing so is one of life's pleasures.

The idea that nothing will mean anything is an inviting thought.

Nicolas Roeg

A New York hotel room: night. A collision of myths. Each person is singular, some of them are lonely. In the night outside, fans crowd the sidewalk and the famous hide out in bars. Four mythical figures meet in a melting pot of the sexual and the cerebral. Accepted notions are reversed: an Actress lectures on scientific theory, a Professor shows her his legs, a powerful Senator confronts his impotence, a Ballplayer displays his tenderness. Memories, childhood and compromise. Bubblegum heroes and basic fears, Hiroshima in New York. Twenty-four frames a second.

Insignificance *came at the right time for me. The overall thought of the piece is that everything is passing. Nothing is forever. The only thing that is forever is hope. I like the way the characters say lightweight things. The Professor sees the truth in a very simple way. The Indian is simplicity itself. All great ideas are simple. It's also about having very little control of things. It touches all kinds of pomposity. Simple truths are reversed and put into the mouths of what appear to be clever people and wise things in the mouths of apparently dumb people. It is all about chance. It changes their lives.*

Nicolas Roeg

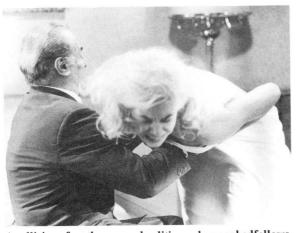

A collision of myths: sex and politics make poor bedfellows.

The Professor carries a torch for The Actress.

I always remebered how I hated fifties' movies. They all seemed so bland then.

I resisted playing her as just a dumb blonde. I tried to achieve moments where everbody knows she is putting it on for the outside world. It's a complete facade.

Theresa Russell

ACTRESS Now the second thing you have to know is that light absolutely always travels at the same speed in all directions at once. A hundred and eighty-six thousand two hundred and eighty-two miles per second.

PROFESSOR Point three nine seven.

ACTRESS It got faster?

PROFESSOR We got more accurate.

My stepfather explained Relativity to me when I was nine. He was an amateur astronomer and he did it through the stars. One night he took me out and said 'Do you see those stars up there? By the time the light from them reaches you they are already going to be gone.' He told me how light takes time to travel. He didn't say it takes one hundred and eighty-six thousand two hundred and eighty-two point two miles per second but he gave me the general idea. So I did understand it before I read the script but I would have explained it like that because that is the way it was told to me.

Theresa Russell

The Actress is pinned to the screen by a determined public and awakes to the knock of Armageddon on the bedroom door. Hiroshima in New York.

'The complete horror and beguilement about even discussing the matter with a serious face is beyond me. Having a son has reinforced my feelings, obviously. Before it was anger and frustration. Now I have the added ingredient of sadness. Because the joy of life is absolutely phenomenal in him,' said Theresa Russell.

The Actress and the Ballplayer. They are tied together by the idea of having a child. This child is famous for being unborn: a myth. The Ballplayer is a lamb in wolf's clothing, a sad and forlorn reminder of a glorious past. The mirror reflects the man, not the myth.

'Hey, Bighitter!'

The script arrived and it said, 'England'. It said 'London, New York' and it had these four great characters. It said 'Nicolas Roeg'. That was enough for me. I've been wanting to work with someone like him for years. Since I started I have always wanted to work with one of the masters. And it seems like the things you do for money don't work out quite as nice as the things you do for fun or love. This turned out to be quite a roller-coaster ride. Jeremy Thomas, the producer, said something pretty neat. He said that he believes that whoever ends up coming to the project – those are the ones who are meant to be involved. It's like water seeking its own level.

I certainly liked the way it was written. The screenplay was lovely. It was like Absurd Theatre. One of my main textbooks a few years ago was Zen and the Art of Archery. *It talked about how to put yourself in a place of purposelessness.* Insignificance *hit the centre of the target each time.*

Gary Busey, the actor and the Ballplayer.

The centre of the target. For the Actress, a family, for the Ballplayer, the home run and an over-whelming number of bubble-gum cards with your own picture on. For the Professor, the relativity of things, and for the Senator, the fixed and absolute notion that there is only one world and that he has defined it.

SENATOR Funny how you talk to a good Jew nowadays, that subject always comes up. Dachau! Same threat to Democracy we're asking you to help fight!

PROFESSOR World War Two had very little to do with communism.

SENATOR Little to do with .... The whole damn thing was a Soviet plot!

PROFESSOR Fifteen million dead Russians, a Soviet plot?

SENATOR They're tricky. Ask yourself this, Professor; what's left of Europe that'll ever be a threat to the Soviets? Round one's theirs, so what do you say?

PROFESSOR I say you ought to see a psychiatrist. Goodnight, Senator.

Tony Curtis, the Senator:

The man has an intensity and glibness – an ability to change and take anything that is given to him and turn it into something positive for himself. I am not that involved politically and never have been. I don't remember too much about the period. There was a lot of acrimony and anger, disappointment and bitterness amongst a lot of people pertaining to Hollywood. But it wasn't just Hollywood.

There is no similarity between us and them. It isn't the real stuff. It is twenty or thirty years later, it has different connotations. The eighties are different from the sixties and fifties, so it is hard to approximate that time. What is easier to do is to take these people out of their time and put them together because they weren't together. If you are dealing with biography you have to deal with reality and a lot of people are nervous about reality. It is someone prepared to talk about what happened in their lives and showing other people in a good light or a bad light. Doing a comedy or doing a drama is the same thing. The emphasis may be on another syllable but that is all it is. You are as close to a joke as you are to a drama.

Drama, comedy, it's all relative. In the film we find both just as we find the co-existence of time: the Hotel and Hiroshima's holocaust.

Int. Corridor. Night.

The SENATOR waits for the elevator, which arrives from below. The INDIAN opens the gates, but before the SENATOR can enter, a small group of JAPANESE PEACE DELEGATES flood out.

ALL PEACE DELEGATES wear lapel badges with a recognizable peace symbol. The SENATOR tenses as they brush past. Then he joins the INDIAN, who closes the gates.

Ext. Hiroshima. Day. (1945)

A JAPANESE WOMAN pats the earth firm around a tiny sapling she has planted by a river, then pours on a little river water from a bowl.

Int. Bathroom. Night.

The PROFESSOR cups his hands full of cold water and ducks his face into them, blowing out. He wipes his dripping face with a white towel.

Shinobu Kanai
A Poison Tree. 'And I water'd it in fears, Night and morning with my tears;' *William Blake.*

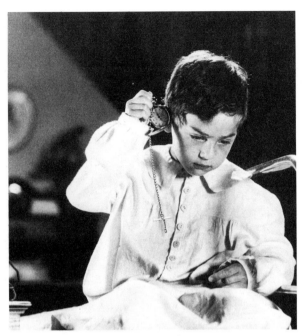

An early experiment with Space-Time.

Michael Emil, the Professor:
I wondered how difficult it would be. If I was playing a lawyer or a criminal or psychiatrist or a businessman or something I could easily have been with some slight variation in my background or personality, it would have been easy. But to be a brilliant Professor is something totally and incredibly different. And on top of that a kind of comic Professor, because the whole thing is a comedy. Yet looking at Nic Roeg's movies, I thought that this is a real challenge for me and if I was going to prove myself then this was the occasion to do it.

The Actress sees a similar challenge and seizes the moment; the Ballplayer sees the past; the Senator sees only what he wants; the Professor perhaps has seen it all.

> PROFESSOR I want to die quietly where I can just slip off the edge of this painful world. Like Columbus never did. Unfortunately. What was it your husband said? If Columbus had slipped up we'd all still be Indians. Cherokee. Instead, what are we? Americans.

Relativity. Communism. Fascism. Protection of Democracy. Theory and explosion. Hiroshima and a Hotel. The night and the stars. Time and myth and insignificance.

> Insignificance ...
> Insignificance (insigni-fikans). 1699. (f. next, or f. In-3 + Significance.) The fact or quality of being insignificant. 1. Want of signification or meaning 1754. 2. Want of significance; unimportance; contemptibility.[9]

Insignificance could be the interplay of bombs and blondes, bubble-gum heroes and civil paranoia. A fantasy encounter between four significant people results in mythical incineration. The laws of probability and the politics of chance create the possible. Chance changes lives and history. The people in a hotel room aren't so special, they just happened to get famous. What they do may change the world; what they are is dust.

The Professor reads the funnies.

BALLPLAYER That's a very big joke. I want to see my wife I just go to the movies. I want to see your underwear, I just walk down to the corner like all the other guys.

ACTRESS I play this girl. She's a what, not a who. She's just a figment of this guy's imagination. He just imagines having me around the place, you know? I spend the entire movie in the tub or in the kitchen or having my skirt blown up around my fucking ears.

ACTRESS Now the second thing you have to know is that light absolutely always travels at the same speed in all directions at once. A hundred and eighty-six thousand two hundred and eighty-two miles per second.
PROFESSOR Point three nine seven.
ACTRESS It got faster?
PROFESSOR We got more accurate.

PROFESSOR World War Two had very little to do with
Communism.

SENATOR Little to do with...! The whole damn thing
was a Soviet plot!

PROFESSOR Fifteen million dead Russians, a Soviet
plot?
SENATOR They're tricky.

ACTRESS I'm trying to tell you how it is I love
you.
BALLPLAYER Not a hell of a lot.
ACTRESS Not how much or how little, how.
BALLPLAYER How?
ACTRESS In my own way.

SENATOR Do you mind if I wait?
ACTRESS Not if you don't mind my throwing up.
SENATOR You've taken a dislike to me I can tell.
It's my fault for bursting in on you like this. You
know, you two could be sisters. Must be kind of
advantageous for a girl like you.

INDIAN I am lift attendant now. I get paycheck,
I eat hotdog. I go up and down.

PROFESSOR I met one of your people once. It was
at Harvard Observatory. In the driveway. He was
collecting garbage. He told me that all true Cherokee
believe wherever they are, there is the centre of the
Universe. Is that so?
INDIAN (nods) But is hard to believe in elevator. I go
up and down. I watch TV. I no longer Cherokee. But I
watch TV. I see your face, I hear your thoughts, and so I
know; you are Cherokee.

I could walk into a little
village that's hardly seen a white man and they'd
say, 'Hey, Bighitter; sit down, have some coffee.'

4

SPIRITS IN THE SKY

1 2 3 4 5 6

INDIAN It is hard to believe in elevator. I go up and down. I watch TV. I no longer Cherokee. But I watch TV.

The only good Indian is a dead Indian. It has to be said that the new Americans, the post-Columbus, non-native Americans, were largely successful in their genocide. Many native Americans live in the USA but their struggle for survival has been not only about flesh and bone but about the spirit, about saving the centre, traditions, culture and a notion of spirituality totally at odds with the growth of the consumer kingdom. MacDonald's has largely replaced Manitou.

The native Americans who adapted and survived lost even as they won, and what was lost was more difficult to reclaim than wealth or power.

I had learned many English words and could recite part of the Ten Commandments. I knew how to sleep on a bed, pray to Jesus, comb my hair, eat with a knife and fork, and use a toilet. I had also learned that a person thinks with his head instead of his heart.[6]

The native American inhabited and created a diversity of cultures, but all were imbued with notions of spirituality and a sense of natural order.

Black Elk, a Holy Man of the Dakota Sioux, travelled through Europe with Buffalo Bill and danced before Queen Victoria. He dictated his autobiography, which became a play and may well soon be a film. He wrote:

You have noticed that everything an Indian does is in a circle, and that is because the Power of the World always works in circles, and everything tries to be round. In the old days when we were a strong and happy people, all our power came to us from the sacred hoop of the nation and so long as the hoop was unbroken the people flourished. The flowering tree was the living centre of the hoop, and the circle of the four quarters nourished it. The east gave peace and light, the south gave warmth, the west gave rain, and the north with its cold and mighty wind gave strength and endurance. This knowledge came to us from the outer world

Commemorative medals like these were given to Indians at treaties or when visiting Washington. Ostensibly a token of peace, the uniformed sleeve clearly indicates the hand of the conqueror.

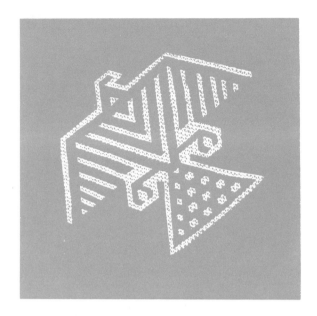

BALLPLAYER I think it's round. Like everything else in nature; the sun, the moon, the flowers, are all based on a circle, you know that? Like the world. I don't know what shape you two geniuses think the world is but me and Columbus think it's round, which is a damn lucky thing for the States because if it wasn't for Columbus we'd all be Indians.

McCarthy's fear of communism was part of the paradox of the American melting pot: that a multi-stranded culture can develop both ghettos and a desperate fear of cultural interchange. The immigrants feared and failed to understand the natives, and undermined and devalued their culture in favour of a culture so disparate in its roots but so determined to develop its own coherence that the only possible result is the simple-minded and bland. The native Americans were steam-rollered to create the triple-thick milkshake and the freeway system. This, apparently, could only be achieved by betrayal.

When President Andrew Jackson suggested in 1829 the enforced repatriation of all the Creeks, Chikasaws, Cherokees, Choctaws and Seminoles beyond the Mississippi, one Creek Indian, Speckled Snake, saw the circle in the motive:

with our religion. Everything the Power of the World does is done in a circle. The Sky is round and I have heard that the Earth is round like a ball and so are all the stars. The Wind, in its greatest power, whirls. Birds make their nests in circles, for theirs is the same religion as ours. The Sun comes forth and goes down again in a circle. The Moon does the same, and both are round.

Even the seasons form a great circle in their changing, and always come back again to where they were. The life of a man is a circle from childhood to childhood and so it is in everything where power moves. Our tipis were round like the nests of birds and these were always set in a circle, the nation's hoop, a nest of many nests where the Great Spirit meant for us to hatch our children.

There is, clearly, an appealing simplicity in such notions. When significance is ascribed to patterns beyond individual control then the individual's insignificance – and accompanying self-doubt – can be earthed. One becomes significant as *part of* the pattern, and hence granted an undeniable destiny.

Brothers! I have listened to many talks from our great father. When he first came over the wide waters, he was but a little man ... very little. His legs were cramped by sitting long in his big boat, and he begged for a little land to light his fire on ... but when the white man had warmed himself before the Indians' fire and filled himself with their hominy, he became very large. With a step he bestrode the mountains, and his feet covered the plains and the valleys. His hand grasped the eastern and the western sea, and his head rested on the moon. Then he became our Great Father. He loved his red children, and he said, 'Get a little further, lest I tread on thee ....'

Brother, I have listened to a great many talks from our great father. But they always began and ended in this – 'Get a little further; you are too near me.' [7]

Pipemen of the year gather to discuss the relative merits of tranquility achieved through inhalation of combustible materials.

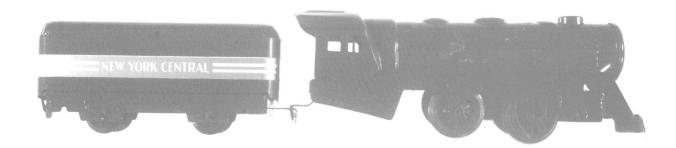

The route which the tribes took when being forced off their land is known to Indians as 'The Trail of Tears'.

Some of the old culture seems not unfamiliar: an oil painting by George Catlin of *Little War*[8] depicts one of the many indigenous ball games played by tribes in the south-eastern USA. Members of different tribes or towns made up two teams. Before and after the game players were subject to rituals and taboos which were similar to those imposed on warriors going into or returning from battle. The game (which is still played by some tribes) is very rough and serious injuries are not uncommon.

Some customs were adopted or adapted and given new twists of meaning. Tribal symbols for war and peace were commonly used by western civilizations in their dealings with Indian tribes. Medals commemorating the inauguration of American Presidents, issued throughout most of the nineteenth century, show both peace pipe and hatchet. They were given to Indians after the signing of treaties or when visiting Washington.

The medal illustrated here shows two hands clasped beneath a crossed pipe and a tomahawk. In order to distinguish the owners of the hands represented, that of the white man is depicted in a uniformed sleeve. And even Indian terminology continues to be used as symbolic codenames in the West. One of the most sophisticated North American nuclear missiles was dubbed the Tomahawk.

No Reservations

When you arise in the morning
Give thanks for the morning light
Give thanks for your life and strength
Give thanks for your food
And give thanks for the joy of living
And if perchance you see no reason for giving thanks
Rest assured the fault is in yourself.

This is from a chant of the Osages, an Indian tribe originating between the Missouri and Arkansas rivers.

CODA 5

1   2   3   4   5   6

I'M SENDING CHESTERFIELDS to all my friends. That's the merriest Christmas any smoker can have—Chesterfield mildness plus no unpleasant after-taste

Ronald Reagan

see RONALD REAGAN starring in "HONG KONG" a Pine-Thomas Paramount Production Color by Technicolor

CHESTERFIELD *Buy the beautiful "Christmas-card" carton*

Prior to his appointment as Chairman of the board, Ronald Reagan courted the media to publicize his views on the burning issues of the day.

**Ballplayers by appointment to the Vatican discuss the
advantages of having God on their side.**

...AND PLAYING BALL

SENATOR Ain't no one going to press the button. We all got too much invested.

In March 1981, when Ronald Reagan was peppered by a would-be assassin, an aide was spotted scrambling about behind his limousine. In his hands was a small, oddly shaped device. This contained the electronic equipment necessary for the President of the United States to launch nuclear weapons and thus start World War Three.

Roger Fisher, a negotiations expert at Harvard Law School, suggested that the bearer of this omni-destructive device should be a volunteer prepared to meet an unpleasant end. Fisher argued that if this kamikaze patriot carried a hatchet with him he could hand it to the President who would then have to hack the bearer to death to take control of the box of tricks himself. He figured that the President would understand the enormity of taking just one life before taking a million.

This idea did not go down at all well with the Pentagon officials who thought it insane to force the President into murdering someone before being able to unleash nuclear weapons. The device is known as 'the football'.

Three minutes to midnight is on the cover of a magazine. Not long after the announcement, in 1949, that the Russians had the bomb, the editors of the *Bulletin of the Atomic Scientists* moved the hands of the clock that regularly appeared on its cover to three minutes to midnight. It was a startling image of the imminence of nuclear war and the Doomsday Clock has been ticking away ever since.

$$E = mc^2$$
$$= \text{Figures in a graveyard}$$
$$MM = 37\text{-}23\text{-}37$$

Or, in the words of the Senator, 'One fuck of a big bang.'

We appeal, as human beings, to human beings: remember your humanity and forget the rest. If you can do so, the way lies open to a new Paradise; if you cannot, there lies before you the risk of universal death.

Albert Einstein

A Plutonium Blonde has risen from the ashes of promise past and is strolling down the centre of a nuclear boulevard, clear in her assumption that the middle of the road is the safest place to be.

She is in no hurry. She has three minutes to spare.

A nuclear bomb was exploded over Hiroshima at 8.15. All subsequent advertisements for clocks and watches in America depicted hands at 8.20. Is there something we should know?

6

THE SCREENPLAY

FADE IN:

EXT. THE UNIVERSE. NIGHT. (1953, UNLESS OTHERWISE STATED)
Open in darkness, but become aware of stars twinkling in the night sky.
MAIN TITLES begin, but very small, white on black in the bottom right-hand corner.

INT. HOTEL ROOM. NIGHT.
Black turns to white. A sheet of calculus fills the screen. An old man's hand adds more figures to it. More TITLES over.

EXT. NEW YORK STREET. NIGHT.
Night sky again, and this time the sound of a film unit shouting, organizing, setting up a shot. The general murmur of a crowd. A lantern on some sort of boom swings lazily across the screen and bleaches us out.

INT. NEW YORK BAR. NIGHT.
A flickering 1950s TV screen fills the screen. The black and white image begins as abstract particles of light.
Distinct forms take shape. A ball in flight. A swinging baseball bat. A man runs backwards to catch a ball...

INT. HOTEL ROOM. NIGHT.
The PROFESSOR's face, suspended in thought.

INT. NEW YORK BAR. NIGHT.
The player on the TV catches his ball neatly.

INT. HOTEL ROOM. NIGHT.
The PROFESSOR completes his thought, smiles and writes.

EXT. NEW YORK STREET. NIGHT.
The film unit preparing for a take. The equipment is being moved around in what seems like confusion. The lights are being centred on an innocent sidewalk grating. We close in on it.

INT. NEW YORK BAR. NIGHT.
The ball game continues on the TV.
Sitting at the bar and watching it is the SENATOR.
He's a fat sweaty man in a fat sweaty suit.
The batsman gets thrown out, the SENATOR finishes his drink in disgust.

INT. HOTEL ROOM. NIGHT.
The PROFESSOR sits alone in the room, surrounded by calculus on the bed, table and floor. There is a pause and stillness as he thinks.
He wipes some sweat from his brow and tries to turn on the small table fan next to him. It doesn't work, though he tries more than once.

INT. BASEMENT. NIGHT.
Beneath the grating, two of the film crew are cramped in the basement with a huge industrial fan. BUD is looking up through the grating. CHARLIE is behind him and can see nothing.

CHARLIE She there?

BUD I can't see.

CHARLIE You can't see nothing?

BUD Just the stars.

CHARLIE Screw the stars.

BUD I like the stars. You look at the stars and you feel like tomorrow you could do anything; kiss that girl, walk on the grass; stars won't think the worse of you. Stars won't even notice. Know what I mean?

CHARLIE She there yet, you philosophical fucking genius?

INT. HOTEL ROOM. NIGHT.
The PROFESSOR moves across and attempts to open the window, but it sticks. He looks out at the city.

EXT. NEW YORK STREET. NIGHT.
A crowd of men push each other in an attempt to get a good view of the filming.

INT. BASEMENT. NIGHT.
The crowd above cheer and applaud.

BUD That's her.

CHARLIE I can't see a fucking thing. If I can't see a fucking thing how do I know when to hit the fan?

A bright light hits the grating from above. A woman's legs appear above the grating; shapely legs in white sandals. A white full-pleated skirt towers up above her calves.

INT. HOTEL. NIGHT.
The PROFESSOR turns from the window having opened it a little. A light white curtain falls in front of it. He turns and surveys his empty room. It is a well-furnished suite with bedroom divided from living area by a light partition, and with a bathroom off the bedroom.
The PROFESSOR wears a crumpled sweatshirt, baggy old suit trousers, and no shoes.
He sighs.

INT. BASEMENT. NIGHT.
BUD and CHARLIE are still in position. Someone unseen shouts at them from above.

VOICE You guys ready?

BUD Yep.

CHARLIE Ready. I was ready last time and the time before that.

VOICE Ready ma'am? OK, this is a take!

The legs walk out of sight for a moment.

EXT. NEW YORK STREET. NIGHT.

Faces in the crowd, mostly male, jostle and gape in anticipation.

INT. BASEMENT. NIGHT.

CHARLIE Let's get it right this time.

BUD I ain't in no hurry.

CHARLIE I hope you go blind.

VOICE Action!

Movement above. The legs appear again.

VOICE And... go fan!

BUD Go.

CHARLIE plugs in the fan. Sparks fly and he shocks himself. The fan spins and roars, messing BUD's hair.

EXT. NEW YORK STREET. NIGHT.
The white pleated skirt flies up in the blast of air.
The crowd can be heard cheering wildly.

INT. HOTEL ROOM. NIGHT.
The PROFESSOR runs his hand through his abundant grey hair. Through the open window he hears the faint sound of a crowd cheering.
The white curtain billows softly in the breeze from the window.

INT. HOSPITAL. DAY.   (1945)
A white sheet is pulled up over a face we hardly glimpse.
The face is Japanese and badly burned, but this is only registered subliminally.
As the sheet settles on the face, a flower of blood appears and grows.

INT. HOTEL ROOM. NIGHT.
The PROFESSOR's bare feet tread carefully through his scattered calculus. He sits and uses one bare toe to pull a sheet before him. He thinks.

EXT. NEW YORK STREET. NIGHT.
The skirt still flies. We recognize the dress.

VOICE OK, cut!

INT. BASEMENT. NIGHT.

BUD Cut it.

CHARLIE gingerly takes out the plug. The fan winds down.

EXT. STREET. NIGHT.
The skirt falls back. The crowd voice disappointment. Her shoes step off the grating.
The crowd still jostle for a better view.
Standing back beyond the crowd is a tall, awkward man. His face is tight and angry as he watches the proceedings.

VOICE All right now, stand back and make way, please gentlemen.

INT. BASEMENT. NIGHT.
The legs disappear.

CHARLIE What'd you see? What'd you see? Did you see anything?

BUD (smiles) I saw the face of God.

INT. NEW YORK BAR. NIGHT.
The men in the bar cheer; someone on the TV has made a home run.
The SENATOR ignores the celebration, takes up his drink, and turns to the man next to him.

SENATOR Did you know that according to the Law of Probability you drink a glass of water and you drink a piece of Napoleon's crap? Perhaps even Mussolini's, but more likely Napoleon's on account of he's been dead longer. Attila the Hun's a dead cert, he's been gone so long. We're all of us part of the same great alimentary fucking canal, you know that?

The man stares at him, too drunk to understand a word. The SENATOR puts on his hat, picks up a bottle of bourbon, and turns to go.
On the TV, a pitcher winds up to throw.

EXT. NEW YORK STREET. NIGHT.
The tall man, an ex-BALLPLAYER, begins to push himself through the crowd. They resist; he pushes harder.
The ACTRESS, whose face we haven't yet seen, is helped to a waiting car. Burly technicians and policemen hold the crowd at bay.
The BALLPLAYER still pushes. The faces of the crowd are angry and unpleasant.
The ACTRESS reaches the car and falls inside.
The BALLPLAYER frees himself from the crowd and a policeman and begins to stride towards the car. Someone tries to stop him, but he brushes them aside.
The car begins to move away. As it passes the crowd, they reach out to touch it, and peer inside for a glimpse of the ACTRESS. All they can see are momentary flashes of her body; a leg her cleavage, her neck.
The BALLPLAYER has almost reached the door of the car when it frees itself from the crowd and begins to accelerate down the street. He too accelerates.
The car goes faster and so does he, until he is running at a good pace.
Through the back window of the car as it pulls away from him, he sees the ACTRESS's face. It is small and frightened, like a rabbit's caught in headlights.
He finds he is not as fit as he used to be and gives up the chase, breathless.

INT. CAR. NIGHT.
The ACTRESS's hands fumble in her bag for dark glasses and a black silk scarf.
The driver watches her in his mirror but catches no glimpse of her face.
Wearing the dark glasses, the ACTRESS puts on her headscarf. The driver, still looking in the mirror, sees an anonymous woman look up at him.

ACTRESS Wherever you're taking me, I don't want to go.

INT. HOTEL CORRIDOR. NIGHT.
The elevator arrives. The doors are opened by an old Indian attendant. The SENATOR emerges and walks just a little unsteadily down the corridor. He finds room no. 1614 and knocks on the door.

INT. HOTEL ROOM. NIGHT.
The PROFESSOR hears the knock. He still sits surrounded by calculus, next to a foot-high pile on the floor.
He gets up and opens the door. The SENATOR stands there beaming.

> *SENATOR* Professor? It's a dog of a night, ain't it? I'm sorry for calling on you so late but I've got something to say to you that's just got to be said before the morning.

The PROFESSOR steps back and he enters.

> Yes sir, it's a dog of a night and tomorrow's going to be a dog of a day. Hey; is this the stuff you hump around with you all the time? Must be quite a few years work right there. I'm not an educated man myself but I'll tell you Professor, I'd give a lot to know all you know. Guess I'm a man who likes to know things.

> *ACTRESS (over)* Do you know where there's a five and dime, an all-night store or something?

INT. CAR. NIGHT.
The car moves through New York. The ACTRESS is leaning forward to speak to the driver.

> *ACTRESS* I need to get some things.

> *DRIVER* Well, I don't know ma'am, they told me I was to...

> *ACTRESS* Well fuck them. Please.

> *DRIVER* Well, I was told...

> *ACTRESS* Please. It's important. Just for me, huh? For me?

Through his mirror the driver can still only see dark glasses.

INT. HOTEL ROOM. NIGHT.
The SENATOR sits in the chair the PROFESSOR had been using.

> *SENATOR* Now the first thing you have to remember is that you ain't on trial. You're not accused of anything. You're not here to be accused. If you feel accused then that makes me an unhappy man. Are you feeling accused?

> *PROFESSOR* No, I am feeling persecuted.

> *SENATOR* Are you now?

> *PROFESSOR* Or have I ever been?

The SENATOR gives a short snort of laughter.

> *SENATOR* That's no accusation, that's an inquiry. Entirely off the record, would you like to tell me what your answer to that question might be? Seems to me there's only Yes or No, but there are some citizens don't like to use either of them words and I'll tell you Professor, they have turned these hearings into one royal pain in the butt. You know the most times one man has cited the Fifth Amendment? Seventy-nine times. He got awful tired. All I'm asking is you give us a straight answer to a straight question tomorrow so's we can all fly home for a long weekend. I haven't seen my wife in a month. Last time I bought a ticket home we had to spend two extra sessions trying that jumped up nigger Robeson for contempt and I missed the damn plane!

The PROFESSOR sits. He suddenly seems older and tireder.

> I came here tonight to make the situation clear. You're not a politician or a military man; you're not used to kicking about in the mud and coming up smelling of roses.

EXT. NEW YORK STREET. NIGHT.
The car pulls up and the ACTRESS jumps out. She runs across the sidewalk to a colourful all-night store.

> *SENATOR (over)* I'd put you in the same category as some of the movie people we've talked to; the type of person to whom mud sticks.

As she reaches the doorway there is a wolf whistle which makes her turn round before she remembers that she's incognito.
The driver looks completely innocent.

INT. HOTEL ROOM. NIGHT.

> *SENATOR* You help us we'll help you come out clean.

> *PROFESSOR* And to come out clean I have to answer Yes?

> *SENATOR* Yes'd be just fine by us. Of course you'd have to couple that with a denunciation of any Communist ideals you once held, and you could show good faith by giving us a few names.

> *PROFESSOR* Is that all?

> *SENATOR* Well, a formal condemnation of the Soviet arms initiative wouldn't do you any harm. I'll tell you in confidence Professor, I don't think these hearings are going to go on for much longer. You could be our last big civilian fish, Professor. And what a fish!

INT. FIVE AND DIME STORE. NIGHT.
The ACTRESS picks out two flashlights and a little toy spaceship.

SENATOR *(over)* You know just about all there is to know about them photons, atomic structure, cosmos, and the Jewish problem. They call you Daddy of the H bomb...

The toys chosen by the ACTRESS are dropped into a white paper bag, making a loud noise.

INT. HOTEL ROOM. NIGHT.
The PROFESSOR closes his eyes.

SENATOR ...and a True Child of the Universe.

The PROFESSOR opens his eyes and looks at the SENATOR sadly.

PROFESSOR In my lifetime I have been accused by the Swiss of being a German Fascist, by the Germans of being a Zionist Conspirator, and by the Americans of being a German Fascist, a Zionist conspirator, and now a Soviet Communist. By two magazines in one week I was called a conscientious objector and a warmonger. Both magazines were reviewing a speech I made to the Mozart Appreciation Society of New England. Now you want to know if I deserve to be called an American.

INT. TRAIN. NIGHT.   (1933)
The PROFESSOR, as a younger man, sits alone in his compartment with a great deal of luggage.
Through the window he watches another train shunt past in the opposite direction. It is loaded to the hilt with silent, ashen refugees.

PROFESSOR *(over)* I tell you, on or off the record, I don't care. I never chose America.

The man in the train looks at his watch. It says 8.15.

INT. HOTEL ROOM. NIGHT.
The PROFESSOR is looking at his watch. It still says 8.15. He closes the watch.

PROFESSOR Had I but known it. I was avoiding Dachau.

INT. FIVE AND DIME. NIGHT.
Two toy trains are thrown into the paper bag, one red, one green. The carriages follow, one by one.

SENATOR *(over)* Funny how you talk to a good Jew nowadays, that subject always comes up. Dachau!

INT. HOTEL ROOM. NIGHT.

SENATOR Same threat to Democracy we're asking you to help fight!

PROFESSOR *(his jaw almost drops)* World War Two had very little to do with Communism.

SENATOR Little to do with...! The whole damn thing was a Soviet plot!

PROFESSOR Fifteen million dead Russians, a Soviet plot?

SENATOR They're tricky.

INT. FIVE AND DIME. NIGHT.
Two or three little toy soldiers are selected from a tangled pile and are dropped in the bag.

SENATOR *(over)* Ask yourself this, Professor; what's left of Europe that'll ever be a threat to the Soviets? Round one's theirs, so what do you say?

INT. HOTEL ROOM. NIGHT.

PROFESSOR I say you ought to see a psychiatrist. Goodnight, Senator.

The PROFESSOR rises. The SENATOR, angered, holds his ground.

SENATOR It'd be a mighty shame if all you stood for was to get muddied up for the sake of haggling over constitutional legalities. I mean don't make the mistake of treating this like a freshman's debate on civil liberties. There are some who've done that and they sounded just fine on the day. One guy got applauded by the fucking stenographer. But he ain't earned jack shit since. Nor has the stenographer. So what about a little co-operation here?

PROFESSOR I can make it very simple. I will not, ever, testify.

SENATOR But you're subpoenaed for tomorrow. We paid for your flight.

PROFESSOR I am here to speak at the Conference for World Peace.

EXT. NEW YORK STREET. NIGHT.
The ACTRESS is at an all-night hamburger stand. Tied to the stand are a bunch of white helium balloons. They bob in the breeze.

PROFESSOR *(over)* The date of my subpoena coincides quite beautifully but it will not prevent me from attending. Nor if I had arranged to go fishing would it have prevented me from catching fish.

She separates three of the balloons and carries them away above her, back to the car.

INT. HOTEL ROOM. NIGHT.

SENATOR You ignore a house committe subpeona and that may be all there is for you to do.

The SENATOR picks up his hat. He nudges the tall pile of calculus with his foot.

> I hear tell you refuse to have copies made of these, now why is that? It'd be a tragedy if they was to go astray.

He moves to the door.

> I'll see you in the morning, Professor. I'll be here around eight to pick you up.
> You'll have to let the peace conference slug it out in your absence. Waste of time anyway; ain't no one going to press no button. We all got too much invested. I mean, think of the real estate.

The PROFESSOR's eyes lift suddenly to stare at the SENATOR.
The SENATOR smiles, opens the door, and leaves.
The PROFESSOR's eyes close tightly and his face gives a nervous twitch. It is a minute gesture that we will become more familiar with; he uses it to avoid thinking.

INT. CAR. NIGHT.
The car is cruising the city. Both the ACTRESS and the DRIVER seem relaxed.
The white balloons bob about on the ceiling of the car.

> DRIVER May I ask you, ma'am, what sort of movie this is you are making?

> ACTRESS A crummy one.

> DRIVER Who is it you play, ma'am?

> ACTRESS I play this girl. She's a what, not a who. She's just a figment of this guy's imagination. He just imagines having me around the place, you know? I spend the entire movie in the tub or in the kitchen or having my skirt blown up around my fucking ears.

EXT. NEW YORK STREET. NIGHT.
From the ACTRESS's point of view we see a row of shop doorways. In each of the doorways stands a prostitute.

> ACTRESS (over) I've been out there since before midnight.

INT. CORRIDOR. NIGHT.
The SENATOR waits for the elevator, which arrives from below.
The INDIAN opens the gates, but before the SENATOR can enter, a small group of JAPANESE PEACE DELEGATES flood out.
ALL PEACE DELEGATES wear lapel badges with a recognizable peace symbol. The SENATOR tenses as they brush past. Then he joins the INDIAN, who closes the gates.

EXT. HIROSHIMA. DAY. (1945)
A JAPANESE WOMAN pats the earth firm around a tiny sapling she has planted by a river, then pours on a little river water from a bowl.

INT. BATHROOM. NIGHT.
The PROFESSOR cups his hands full of cold water and ducks his face into them, blowing out. He wipes his dripping face with a white towel.

INT. CAR. NIGHT.
The ACTRESS lies back in the seat and becomes silent, or perhaps hums quietly to herself.
She pulls down one of the balloons and absent-mindedly caresses it's surface, very much like a two-year-old might.

INT. DORMITORY. NIGHT.   (1931)
It is the early thirties. A thin five-year-old runs terrified down a row of institutional beds, pursued by a band of other girls. They bundle her onto a bed and she disappears beneath them.
Lots of hands of different sizes clutch her tiny arm and tear from her wrist a simple little watch.

INT. CAR. NIGHT.
A scarlet finger nail presses into the fleshy surface of a balloon.

INT. DORMITORY. NIGHT.   (1931)
A tall, lanky girl holds the watch out of reach. The small girl reaches up for it hopelessly.

INT. CAR. NIGHT.
The nail presses further into the balloon until it seems it must burst.

INT. DORMITORY. NIGHT.   (1931)
The tall girl throws the watch from an open window out into the night.

EXT. UNIVERSE. NIGHT.   (1931)
The watch falls through the night sky.

INT. CAR. NIGHT.
The fingernail changes direction and emerges from the balloon, which stays intact.
The ACTRESS lets it float back up.

> ACTRESS Do you have a watch?

> DRIVER Yeh, I have a watch.

INT. HOTEL ROOM. NIGHT.
The PROFESSOR winds his watch. It still says 8.15.

> DRIVER *(over)* It's about 2.30 in the morning.

> ACTRESS *(over)* Don't tell me the time! I don't want to know.

He closes the watch.

INT. CAR. NIGHT.

> ACTRESS Can I borrow it? Please? I can let you have it back tomorrow.

EXT. ORPHANAGE. NIGHT.   (1931)
The watch hits a metal grating and disappears through it.

> ACTRESS *(over)* Here. Stop here. Stop here.

INT. HOTEL ROOM. NIGHT.
The PROFESSOR leans back and closes his eyes.
He lies on his bed, fully dressed, and crosses his hands on his chest like a contented corpse.
The room is still. Street sounds can be heard in the distance. The light white curtains billow softly.

EXT. LAKE. DAY.   (1933)
White sails billow.

INT. HOTEL ROOM. NIGHT.
From beyond the window a red neon light flashes lazily onto the curtains.

EXT. LAKE. DAY.   (1933)
The PROFESSOR, as a younger man, sits beneath the sails in a small boat, fishing.

INT. HOTEL ROOM. NIGHT.
A breeze from the window disturbs a few sheets of calculus, but the PROFESSOR has used his shoes as paperweights.

EXT. LAKE. DAY.   (1933)
Sails billow.
The PROFESSOR, slightly less young, watches from the shore as his boat is sailed away from him by a group of Nazi Stormtroopers. They are bad sailors. One trips.
He smiles.
They rip the sail, he stops smiling. They begin to vandalize the boat.
There is a knock on the door.

INT. HOTEL ROOM. NIGHT.
The PROFESSOR's eyes open. He props himself up.

> PROFESSOR Who is it?

> ACTRESS *(from outside)* You wouldn't believe me.

The PROFESSOR struggles up, looks at his alarm clock which reads 2.45, and goes to the door. The ACTRESS stands there with her bag and balloons, still in disguise.

> ACTRESS Hi.

> PROFESSOR Hello.

> ACTRESS Are you busy? Only I'm probably being pursued. This is an awful liberty I know, but I'm very honoured to meet you.

> PROFESSOR Who is pursuing you?

> ACTRESS Just about everybody. I thought you'd be asleep. It's almost three. Would you like me to go?

> PROFESSOR No, please.

He gestures her in. She enters and he closes the door. They both stand awkwardly.

> ACTRESS I had to come and see you before you fly home or I fly west and I've hardly had a moment; I've been shooting all week. My movie.

She undoes her scarf and removes her dark glasses, then stands there expectantly. He looks at her steadily. A pause.

> ACTRESS You don't recognize me do you?

> PROFESSOR Umm... no.

> ACTRESS That's wonderful.

Another awkward pause.

> ACTRESS Have I interrupted your work?

> PROFESSOR No, just some calculations.

> ACTRESS What are you trying to calculate?

She crouches down near the main pile of paper. Her hand reaches out to touch it gently.

> PROFESSOR I'm trying to Unify the Fields.

> ACTRESS Will it take long?

> PROFESSOR Another four years perhaps.

> ACTRESS Gee.

She stands again. There is yet another awkward pause.

> PROFESSOR You are an actress?

> ACTRESS Mmmhmm.

> PROFESSOR What is your name?

She crosses to the window and points out in the direction of the flashing red neon. He comes to join her.

EXT. NEW YORK STREET. NIGHT.
*High above the street. In the foreground part of a huge neon sign,
but too close for any letters to be readable.*
*In the distance, the hotel, with few windows lit. Two figures at
one window.*

> *PROFESSOR (over)* Ahah. I've heard of her. Is she
> good?

> *ACTRESS (over)* She tries hard.

INT. HOTEL ROOM. NIGHT.

> *PROFESSOR* Why is she here?

> *ACTRESS* A visit.

> *PROFESSOR* Why?

> *ACTRESS* You're famous.

> *PROFESSOR* So are you.

> *ACTRESS* I know. We have an awful lot in
> common.

INT. SENATOR'S ROOM. NIGHT.
A smaller room in the same hotel.
*The SENATOR lies on his bed without his jacket. He counts the
money in his wallet with one hand while holding the phone in the
other.*

> *SENATOR* And who else?

He throws his wallet onto the table. A photograph falls out of it.

> *SENATOR* Who else?

*The photograph shows a fat woman in thin slacks flanked by two
revolting children pulling faces, tongues out.*

> *SENATOR* And how much?

INT. HOTEL ROOM. NIGHT.

> *PROFESSOR* Because of being famous, every-
> where I go people fall over themselves to be with
> me, like a troupe of clowns chasing an old
> automobile. Because of fame, everything I do
> develops into a ridiculous comedy.

> *ACTRESS* You're lucky. Everything I do develops
> into a nightmare. People keep throwing them-
> selves in front of me and I daren't stop.

The PROFESSOR sits down amidst the calculus.

> Have I disturbed you?

> *PROFESSOR* No, no.

> *ACTRESS* Shall I go?

96

PROFESSOR No, no, no.

Yet another awkward pause.

ACTRESS It's late. I just spent four hours of my life having my skirt blown up around my ears. They fixed up a fan beneath a grating out on Fifty-Third. Whoosh. All night long. Do you ever get the feeling it might be later than you think? Anyway, I knew my last chance to see you before you flew away or I died from intimate exposure would be to wake you up in the middle of the night and I told myself go ahead, because if he doesn't understand how you have to wake people up in the middle of the night sometimes, nobody will. I thought what the hell! Have you ever noticed how what the hell is always the right decision? What did you do tonight?

PROFESSOR I, er, arrived, then washed, then attempted to derive the tangential vector quantities for alpha C^2 when the value for T is infinity.

ACTRESS You had a bad night too, huh?

PROFESSOR I suppose so. I could have been watching a pretty girl having her skirt blown up around her ears.

ACTRESS Would you have watched?

PROFESSOR Would you have liked me to?

ACTRESS (thinks) Yes. It would have embarrassed me. The others didn't embarrass me.

She looks towards the window.

EXT. NEW YORK STREET. NIGHT.
The neon sign still flashes laconically.

ACTRESS (over) I don't think a girl should go through a thing like that without feeling embarrassed.

INT. LOCKER ROOM. NIGHT.   (1938)
In a dark room, three twelve-year-old boys turn on their flashlights and all point them in the same direction.

ACTRESS (over) It doesn't seem natural somehow.

INT. SENATOR'S ROOM. NIGHT.
The SENATOR thumbs through the pages of a lurid movie magazine.
Established personalities show their teeth and their cleavages.
Unestablished starlets have been persuaded to show more.

PROFESSOR (over) How could I have embarrassed you when they could not?

ACTRESS They saw a Star doing glamourous

things right there on the block. You'd have seen a girl flashing her legs for a bunch of jerks.

INT. HOTEL ROOM. NIGHT.
The ACTRESS comes across to the PROFESSOR's chair.

ACTRESS Look. Could I explain something to you?

PROFESSOR Certainly.

Another pause.

PROFESSOR What?

ACTRESS The Theory of Relativity.

PROFESSOR All of it?

ACTRESS Just the Specific. The General Theory is a bit too complicated to go into this late don't you think? Please? I'll never have another chance to prove it.

PROFESSOR Why do you have to prove it? You know what you know.

ACTRESS But you don't believe me.

PROFESSOR If you say you understand Relativity then I believe you.

ACTRESS You're just saying that to avoid seeing me embarrass myself.

PROFESSOR Of course not.

ACTRESS You honestly believe I understand Relativity?

PROFESSOR Yes.

ACTRESS Swear to God?

PROFESSOR Whose God?

ACTRESS Yours.

PROFESSOR Prove it. With my God you take no chances.

He picks up a pad and pencil from the floor and offers it to her. She reacts as though he was trying to hand her a live snake.

ACTRESS No, no, no. I'm not theoretical, I demonstrate. I bought a few things.

She tips out her purchases onto the floor. The balloons for the moment have disappeared.
The toys land in a heap, tangled.

EXT. HIROSHIMA. DAY. (1945)
A woman's straight black hair hangs from the door of a wrecked streetcar. An advertisement for a Japanese brand of hair oil is pasted to the side of the streetcar and is burning. Only her hair is visible; the rest of her is buried under rubble.
The image is momentary.

INT. HOTEL ROOM. NIGHT.
The ACTRESS flicks back a few locks of blonde hair that have fallen over her brow.

ACTRESS First of all you have to know two things.

She takes two books; The Brothers Karamazov *and* Jane Eyre.

ACTRESS The first thing is if you drop a copy of *The Brothers Karamazov* in a moving train it doesn't fly backwards and flatten the conductor.

She throws it behind her horizontally. It hits the wall and drops to the floor.

It drops relative to the train.

She drops Jane Eyre *straight onto the floor.*

So if anybody does any experiments on a moving train or in a laboratory in Princeton the results will always be the same because wherever his springs and rulers and balls are, he's there too. That's the first thing you have to know.

She finds one of the flashlights.

Now the second thing you have to know is that light absolutely always travels at the same speed in all directions at once. A hundred and eighty-six thousand two hundred and eighty-two miles per second.

PROFESSOR Point three nine seven.

ACTRESS It got faster?

PROFESSOR We got more accurate.

ACTRESS Then don't confuse me.

She takes a toy soldier and a toy car and demonstrates on the carpet as she speaks.

ACTRESS Now we have to imagine a man in a car travelling at thirty miles an hour and a hiker standing by the road waiting for a lift. The driver as he drives up at thirty miles an hour throws a stone at the hiker at another thirty miles an hour. He's a league pitcher. So the question is if the car is travelling at thirty miles an hour and the stone is thrown in front of it at thirty miles an hour what is the speed of the stone when it hits the hiker?

Answer, sixty miles an hour. Pretty straightforward. But let's forget the stone and instead imagine the man in the car flashing his headlights to tell the hiker to get the hell out of the way. Does the light from the headlamps travel towards the hiker at a hundred and eighty-six thousand two hundred and eighty-two point...

PROFESSOR Three nine seven.

ACTRESS ...miles per second plus thirty miles an hour? Answer, no! Because the speed of light is always the same. Did you ever prove that hypothesis?

PROFESSOR It was never disproved.

ACTRESS Let's hope it never is.

PROFESSOR Amen.

She discards her soldier and car.

ACTRESS Now then. Here we go.

She finds the two toy trains and sets them up.

We have to imagine two locomotives speeding past each other at a hell of a speed. A red one and a green one. Now the driver of each train has a flashlight which he turns on at the precise moment they pass each other.

She pushes the trains past each other. When they are level she flashes the flashlight.

Now the light from the flashlight travels at the same speed regardless of the speeds of the flashlights themselves, so both flashes expand together in all directions just like...

She reaches up, takes a dangling string, and pulls down one of the balloons.

...a single sphere of light.

She holds the balloon six inches off the floor, between the trains.

Now the driver of the red locomotive watches the light spread out at the same speed in all directions at once and regardless of the fact that he's moving very fast thataway...

She moves the red train on.

He stays with the centre of the sphere of light that came from his flashlight, both flashlights.

She moves the balloon to hover over the red train.

And if he looks over at the green locomotive he'll see that the driver on the green train has moved

thataway...

She moves the green train on in its own direction.

...and is therefore not in the centre of the light anymore. I know you're way ahead of me.

The PROFESSOR smiles, distant.

ACTRESS Everything's just fine until you look at it from the point of view of the driver of the green train because he sees the same thing. He flashed too, remember.

The ACTRESS has returned the trains to their positions alongside one another and the balloon between them.
She moves the red train in the other direction.

ACTRESS So both drivers think they're the ones in the centre of the light while the other driver has moved on past.
Question: which one of them is right?
Answer:

She plucks down a second balloon.

Both of them.

She weights the balloons down with the trains.

Not only that. I figured out what would happen if you just stood on the tracks and watched. The trains would both vamoose...

She plucks the third balloon down for herself.

...the light would stay with you, and you'd be right too.

PROFESSOR That's remarkably...

ACTRESS That's not all.

She switches on the trains. They chug off, pulling their balloons.

ACTRESS If we stand on the tracks a little longer you know what happens?

PROFESSOR We get run over?

He chuckles. She doesn't find it amusing.

PROFESSOR I'll stay behind afterwards and clean the board.

She is embarrassed. The trains chug further away.

ACTRESS I don't like to be patronized.

One of the trains hits the PROFESSOR's discarded shoe and can go no further.

PROFESSOR I'm sorry.

ACTRESS Anyway, it's not just speed and distances.

She squeezes and bursts her balloon.

EXT. ORPHANAGE. NIGHT. (1931)
The watch disappears down the grating.

ACTRESS (over) It's Time as well.

INT. HOTEL ROOM. NIGHT.

ACTRESS Have you got a watch? We have to use it.

The PROFESSOR gets out his watch. It still says 8.15.
The ACTRESS turns off the light. She hands him a flashlight, which he turns on, and turns one on herself.

ACTRESS We have to imagine this room is the Universe. We begin together somewhere in Space-Time and we synchronize at ...what? What does you watch say?

PROFESSOR Eight fifteen?

ACTRESS Right. Eight fifteen.

She sets her borrowed watch by the light of the flashlight.

INT. CHILD'S BEDROOM. DAY. (1890)
A YOUNG BOY sits up in bed playing with a home-made electromagnet. He uses it to pick up his special brand new fob watch, then lets it drop.

ACTRESS (over) Now I travel away from you at a hell of a speed, say one fifth the speed of light and I travel for five minutes and it gets me...

INT. HOTEL ROOM. NIGHT.
The ACTRESS opens the connecting doors and clambers up onto the bed, quite a way from him.

ACTRESS ...here. Now my watch says twenty past eight but it isn't very reliable so I look across the Universe to check by your watch and what does it say?

She points her light at him. He looks at his watch.

INT. CHILD'S BEDROOM. DAY.   (1890)
The watch jumps up, falls back.

INT. HOTEL ROOM. NIGHT.

PROFESSOR Twenty past eight.

ACTRESS Not to me it doesn't, it says nineteen minutes past eight because twenty minutes past eight hasn't reached me yet.

The beam from her flashlight slowly crosses the room from him to her, briefly illuminating the trains, the calculus, a balloon.

It takes a minute for me to see your watch because light is taking a minute to get here, see?

INT. CHILD'S BEDROOM. DAY.   (1890)
The boy shakes his watch and puts it to his ear, but, sadly, it is broken.

ACTRESS (over) So your watch is getting slower and slower!

The watch says 8.15.

INT. HOTEL ROOM. NIGHT.

ACTRESS Now here comes the thousand dollar question.

She points her flashlight at her own face.

Remember if you look at my watch it's going to take a minute to reach you too. So what do you say my watch says?

PROFESSOR Nineteen minutes past eight.

The PROFESSOR turns his flashlight from his watch to her face, which becomes doubly illuminated.

ACTRESS Which means I say you're going more slowly than me while you say I'm going more slowly than you.

The room is lit by the occasional flash of the red neon and the light from her face.

INT. LOCKER ROOM. NIGHT.   (1938)
The twelve-year-old boys point their flashlights.
On a bench opposite them a twelve-year old girl sits in her nightdress. The flashlights move down from her face and explore her body. They focus in her lap.
She lifts her nightdress. The boys gaze intently.

INT. HOTEL ROOM. NIGHT.
The PROFESSOR still has his light on her face.

PROFESSOR Beautiful.

ACTRESS Isn't it.

She stands and moves across to turn on the light.

ACTRESS So.

She switches it on. It hurts her eyes.

INT. AUDITION ROOM. DAY.   (1945)
In a seedy room, too brightly lit, a row of young girls including the ACTRESS, but with dark hair, stand facing two fat men.
At an unseen signal the girls lift their skirts to display their legs, each girl to a different height, depending on her modesty, or lack of it.

ACTRESS (over) So given a constant frame of reference within which to experiment according to Galileo's original principles...

INT. HOTEL ROOM. NIGHT.

ACTRESS ...and accepting the hypothesis that light always travels at a hundred and eighty-six thousand two hundred and eighty-two point... three nine seven miles per second in all directions at once, then the main point I have demonstrated is that all measurements of Time and Space are necessarily made Relative to the observer and are not necessarily the same for two independent observers.
That is the Specific Theory of Relativity.
Isn't it?

PROFESSOR Yes it is

She laughs with relief and falls back onto the floor or, preferably, the bed. She rolls around onto her stomach and rests her chin on her hands.

ACTRESS Now you have to show me your legs.

He smiles, leans down, and begins to roll up his trousers.

INT. AUDITION ROOM. DAY.   (1945)
The row of girls stand with their skirts raised.
The ACTRESS looks surreptitiously left and right and then raises her skirt to her waist, higher than any of the other girls.

INT. HOTEL ROOM. NIGHT.
The PROFESSOR's trousers stay rolled up above his knees.

PROFESSOR I promise never to display these in public if you promise never to lecture in nuclear physics.

ACTRESS I couldn't if I wanted to. It's one thing remembering it; I only wish I understood it all.

PROFESSOR You learned it without understanding it?

ACTRESS Mmmmm. It's like riding on the subway; I know where I get on and where to get off but while I'm travelling I don't know where the hell I am. I suppose you must, but then you dug all the tunnels. Still, I know the premise and the results, that's the main thing.

PROFESSOR That's nothing.

ACTRESS I'm sorry?

The mood changes. He becomes very serious.

PROFESSOR If I told you the moon is made of cheese, would you believe me?

ACTRESS No.

PROFESSOR If I told you it was made of sand?

ACTRESS Maybe.

EXT. BEACH OR LAKESIDE. DAY.   (1950)
It is evening. A group of scientific types, all men, stroll along the shore in animated conversation.
A little way behind them and far more thoughtful is the PROFESSOR.

PROFESSOR (over) If I told you I knew for certain?

ACTRESS (over) I'd believe you.

PROFESSOR (over) So now you know the moon is made of sand.

ACTRESS (over) Yes.

INT. HOTEL ROOM. NIGHT.

PROFESSOR But it isn't.

ACTRESS But I only said I knew because you said you knew!

PROFESSOR But I lied. Knowledge is not truth. It is merely mindless agreement.

EXT. BEACH OR LAKESIDE. DAY.   (1950)
All the men are wearing unsuitable dark shoes.
The trousers of their suits are getting wet and covered in sand, their shoes messier.

PROFESSOR (over) You agree with me, I agree with someone else; we all have knowledge, but we get no closer to the truth of the moon.

Only the PROFESSOR, yards behind them, has bare feet and his trousers rolled up.

PROFESSOR (over) We can never understand a thing by agreeing, by making definitions; only by

turning over the possibilities. It's called thinking.

The PROFESSOR stands alone, looking out to sea. It is still light, but a crescent moon is up.

PROFESSOR (over) If I say I know, I stop thinking, but so long as I think I come to understand, I might approach some Truth.

INT. HOTEL ROOM. NIGHT.
The ACTRESS is entranced.

ACTRESS This is the best conversation I ever had.

He smiles, tired. His eyes close.

INT. STUDY. NIGHT.   (1950)
The PROFESSOR, home from the beach, sits at a mahogony desk. He removes his shoe so that both feet are bare (he wears no socks) and lifts it to the desk.
He carefully pours a quantity of sand from it.
The sand falls, as from an hourglass, onto the calculus in front of him.

ACTRESS (over) Is it over?

INT. HOTEL ROOM. NIGHT.
He opens his eyes. He is very tired.

PROFESSOR I think it had better be.

She stands, he follows. They find her coat in silence and he holds it out for her to put on, but instead she turns and takes it from him.

ACTRESS A girlfriend and I played a game a few years back. We each made a list of the men it would be nicest to sleep with. You came third on mine.

PROFESSOR Third?

ACTRESS Then I figured out how old you are.

PROFESSOR And you struck me off?

ACTRESS No. I moved you to the top.

There is an awkward pause. The PROFESSOR can't think of a thing to say.

INT. SENATOR'S ROOM. NIGHT.
There is a knock on the door. The SENATOR, in shirtsleeves, opens it.
His face registers surprise. He smiles with far too much charm.

INT. HOTEL ROOM. NIGHT.

PROFESSOR Well, thank you. But no thank you.

He moves away.

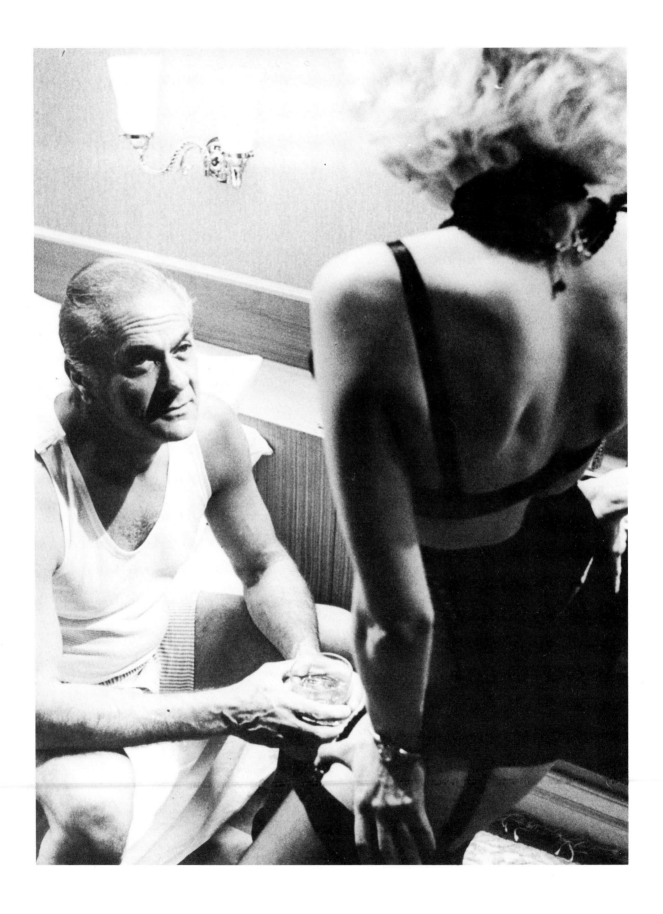

ACTRESS But er... you can't just throw me onto the streets at this hour.

PROFESSOR I suppose not. You are welcome to stay.

She smiles.

PROFESSOR I shall sleep in the bathtub.

He begins to gather some sheets from the bed.

ACTRESS Don't be absurd.

PROFESSOR A fine American tradition.

ACTRESS You can't sleep in the bathtub.

PROFESSOR What's good enough for Cary Grant is good enough for me.

As he passes her with the sheets to go into the bathroom, she grabs them so that he has to stop. They hold the sheets between them.

ACTRESS We don't have to make love. Wouldn't it be nice just to share the bed?

PROFESSOR Perhaps I could give you my telephone number. You'd be welcome to visit me at my home.

ACTRESS You'd never find time for me. I'd just end up on first name terms with your telephone service.

PROFESSOR I have no service. I have a secretary whose first name is a mystery to me. I have a small house on a large river full of fish, which I can't catch, and I have a great deal of time to offer.

She drops her end of the bedding. Looks a little embarrassed, a little ashamed.

ACTRESS I'm sorry. I have none to offer you beyond tonight. I hoped we could just... come together, you know, in the middle of all this, for an hour or so.

PROFESSOR Then don't go.

She smiles.

PROFESSOR But I sleep in the bathtub.

He walks past her, but she stops him.
She stands between him and the bathroom door.
He drops the sheets and goes back to his work, sitting down and picking up calculus.
She wanders over.

INT. SENATOR'S ROOM. NIGHT.
The SENATOR sits on his bed in his shorts.

A blonde with her back to us slips off her clothes.
He examines her body, chewing his lip. He drinks some whisky and smiles nervously, almost shyly.

ACTRESS (over) You're calculating the Shape of Space, right?

INT. HOTEL ROOM. NIGHT.

PROFESSOR Yes.

She kneels beside him.

ACTRESS When you've finished this you will have expressed the precise nature of the physical universe, right?

PROFESSOR So?

She takes the pages out of his hand.

ACTRESS So do it tomorrow. It'll be here. I won't.

INT. SENATOR'S ROOM. NIGHT.
The blonde moves towards him. She takes his glass out of his hand and puts it onto the table. She moves in an arch sexual way, reminiscent of Monroe in the tackier movies.

INT. HOTEL ROOM. NIGHT.
The PROFESSOR has stood and moved away.
He picks up the bedding and disappears into the bathroom.
The ACTRESS, left alone, wanders to the window where she is illuminated by the neon.

ACTRESS I wish they'd switch me off.

He returns without the bedding.

PROFESSOR I prefer to look up.

ACTRESS Stars? Stars are too far away. They make me feel small and lonely.

PROFESSOR Me too. All who look feel small and lonely as the rest. Doesn't that make you feel better?

ACTRESS A little.

PROFESSOR Well then.

ACTRESS Well then what?

PROFESSOR Well then, what the hell.

He returns to the bathroom.

INT. BATHROOM. NIGHT.
The PROFESSOR plucks the bedding from the bathtub.

INT. HOTEL ROOM. NIGHT.

He emerges. She laughs with glee.
He throws the bedding up into the air and onto the bed.
A sheet billows.

INT. SENATOR'S ROOM. NIGHT.

The SENATOR is making love to the prostitute, although not actually screwing. The glimpses we catch of her all seem to confirm that it's Monroe.
She is far more active than he is.

INT. HOTEL ROOM. NIGHT.

The PROFESSOR and the ACTRESS sit with their backs to each other on opposite sides of the bed.
We see them in long shot, and there is something odd about it. All their movements for the next few scenes seem slower than is natural.
She is taking off a shoe. The PROFESSOR picks up his Alarm clock and winds it. The winding up of the clock is what marginally winds down the pace of reality.

> PROFESSOR Is it late or early?

> ACTRESS It's relative.

He turns to look at her with a slight grimace on his face.
She turns to look at him with a slight look of apology on her face. Small and timid.
The PROFESSOR's point of view of her face.

EXT. NEW YORK STREET. NIGHT.

The BALLPLAYER's face. Hard as rock, his breathing heavy. The car drives away from him. The ACTRESS's face framed in the rear window, small and frightened.
We watch the car until it turns out of sight.
The BALLPLAYER catches his breath and gives a cough. He turns and walks away from us.
A broad man in a loud jacket, who was cheering earlier, comes up to him waving a scrap of paper and a pencil.

> PUNTER Boy, what a night, huh? Would you mind?

The BALLPLAYER knocks the paper and pencil out of his hand and walks by him. He moves against the dispersing crowd.

INT. HOTEL ROOM. NIGHT.

Unnatural pace. Long shot.
The ACTRESS and the PROFESSOR as before.

> ACTRESS Your watch is just there.

> PROFESSOR It hasn't told me the time since I was eleven years old.

> ACTRESS Did you drop it?

> PROFESSOR No, I picked it up, with a large electromagnet.

She slowly removes her borrowed watch, almost like striptease, and leans across the bed, dangling it.

INT. RESTAURANT. NIGHT.   (1953)

A beautiful watch, with a jewelled face and a sparkling diamanté strap is passed across a superbly laid table.
The brawny hand of the BALLPLAYER fumbles a little, but slips the watch onto the ACTRESS'S delicate wrist.

EXT. NEW YORK STREET. NIGHT.

On a much quieter street, the BALLPLAYER walks with his hands in his pockets, very depressed. He comes to the entrance of a bar, pauses, then goes in.
He almost bumps into the SENATOR on his way out.

INT. HOTEL ROOM. NIGHT.

Unnatural pace. Long shot.
The ACTRESS takes off her other shoe. The PROFESSOR sets his clock.

INT. NEW YORK BAR. NIGHT.

BALLPLAYER sits drinking orange juice, which is no help. The baseball game is still on TV, but he barely watches it.
He stares instead at a movie calender hanging on the other side of the bar. The ACTRESS smiles at him, barely dressed.

INT. SENATOR'S ROOM. NIGHT.

The SENATOR rolls over and lies on his back like a stranded whale. It's as if he's in pain.
The PROSTITUTE leans up on one arm and reaches down for his flaccid penis, attempting to bring it to life.

> PROSTITUTE Take your time honey, there's plenty of time.

INT. NEW YORK BAR. NIGHT.

The BALLPLAYER reaches over and pulls down the calender. He tears it in half carefully, then quarters, then eigths...

INT. SENATOR'S ROOM. NIGHT.

The PROSTITUTE goes down on him.
He closes his eyes tight.

INT. NEW YORK BAR. NIGHT.

The BALLPLAYER has turned the calender to confetti, which he lets snow onto the bar.

INT. HOTEL ROOM. NIGHT.

Unnatural pace. Long shot.
A breeze from the window ripples the calculus.
The ACTRESS puts her shoes together tidily.
They sit on opposite sides of the bed, hands in laps.

INT. NEW YORK BAR. NIGHT.

BALLPLAYER opens a pack of gum, looks at card and flips it into the confetti despondently. Into the bar comes the DRIVER, obviously looking for him.

INT. HOTEL ROOM. NIGHT.

Unnatural pace. Long shot.
The PROFESSOR, plucking up courage, stands and takes off his trousers. He still wears his shirt, sweatshirt, and underpants.

EXT. HOTEL ENTRANCE. NIGHT.

The BALLPLAYER gets out of the car seen earlier. The DRIVER leans out of the window as he heads for the hotel lobby.

DRIVER And she took my damn watch.

INT. HOTEL ROOM. NIGHT.
Unnatural pace. Long shot.
The ACTRESS stands and turns. She looks at the PRO-FESSOR and he looks down at his legs. Shrugs.
She raises her arms to unclip her dress at the neck.
He looks away.

INT. SENATOR'S ROOM. NIGHT.
The SENATOR lies staring upwards, his face sweaty and distressed.
The PROSTITUTE disengages herself from him and disappears.

INT. ELEVATOR. NIGHT.
The BALLPLAYER stands in one corner of the elevator, the INDIAN in another.
The INDIAN grins at his passenger and, taking an imaginary little baseball bat, gives a little swing, then nods his head in question.
The BALLPLAYER considers, then shakes his head. His expression never changes.
He opens more gum, checks the card and flips it.
The doors open.

INT. HOTEL ROOM. NIGHT.
Unnatural pace, but slightly different. Long shot.
The PROFESSOR puts down his clock. The ACTRESS tidies her shoes. They sit on opposite sides of the bed, hands in laps.
The PROFESSOR, plucking up courage, stands and takes off his trousers.
The ACTRESS stands and turns. She looks at the PROFESSOR and he looks down at his legs. Shrugs.
She raises her arms to unclip her dress at the neck.
He looks away, then looks back. Smiles.
There is an extremely loud knocking on the door.

INT. CORRIDOR. NIGHT.
The BALLPLAYER hits the door four times.

BALLPLAYER Open the door you dumb broad; I know you're in there!

INT. HOTEL ROOM. NIGHT.
Pace back to normal.
However this is not particularly discernable as the PROFESSOR and the ACTRESS have frozen in surprise.
They whisper.

PROFESSOR Who is it?

ACTRESS Just a fan.

PROFESSOR Do all your fans follow you so persistently?

ACTRESS Only those I marry.

INT. CORRIDOR. NIGHT.

BALLPLAYER You want me to get a pass key? I only have to sign my name and the night man would open this door damn fast, you know that.

ACTRESS No..!

INT. HOTEL ROOM. NIGHT.

PROFESSOR He is famous?

The ACTRESS struggles into her shoes.

ACTRESS He hit home safely in fifty-six games with an average of a hundred and thirty-five. He's God.

A bang on the door. She runs around collecting her things.

PROFESSOR Should I let him in?

ACTRESS No, he's angry.

PROFESSOR You think if we keep the door closed he'll get happy?

She heads for the bathroom.

BALLPLAYER (*from outside*) You hiding yourself in the john? I'm going to look in the john. There's no place to hide.

She sits down on the bed and lets her things drop. There are more bangs on the door.

ACTRESS I think he's just angry, not livid, the way he's banging.

PROFESSOR How can you tell?

ACTRESS He's not using his head.
Another thump. The PROFESSOR goes to the door.

PROFESSOR I go talk to him.

He almost opens the door, but another thump from outside dissuades him. He straightens with dignity, unaware that he has no trousers on.

PROFESSOR Ya, was ist das denn, was kann ich für ihn machen?

INT. CORRIDOR. NIGHT.

BALLPLAYER So you finally slept with the delicatessen. You speak English?

INT. HOTEL ROOM. NIGHT.

PROFESSOR Ich kann nicht lügen. Yes, I do.

The ACTRESS sits on the bed with her face in her hands.

BALLPLAYER (over) So is my wife in there with you? If she's not there then you tell me and as a man of honour I'll believe you and leave you to sleep. I'll tell you what I'm going to do. I'm going to count to ten.

The ACTRESS looks up and grimaces slightly.

INT. CORRIDOR. NIGHT.
The BALLPLAYER counts to himself; one, two...

INT. HOTEL ROOM. NIGHT.
The ACTRESS gets up, strides to the door and yells.

ACTRESS You never counted past three in your life you dumb ox!

INT. CORRIDOR. NIGHT.

BALLPLAYER Shit.

INT. HOTEL ROOM. NIGHT.

ACTRESS One two three home; that's as far as you bothered to go.

A thump, then another, and another. They sound like they could go on all night.

ACTRESS I'm going to let him in. Lock yourself in the bathroom.

PROFESSOR Certainly not.

She puts a safety chain on the door and opens it. She and the BALLPLAYER look at each other for a long time. The PROFESSOR wanders away.

BALLPLAYER (through open door) OK. I ain't angry with you. I'm just a little disappointed.

INT. CORRIDOR. NIGHT.

The ACTRESS's face is only half visible through the door.

ACTRESS Listen. If you so much as make a move towards the man I'm with I'll be in that elevator and that's the last you'll see of me for a very long time.

INT. HOTEL ROOM. NIGHT.
The BALLPLAYER's face through the door.

BALLPLAYER That's a very big joke. I want to see my wife I just go to the movies. I want to see your underwear, I just walk down to the corner like all the other guys.

ACTRESS Be warned.

She lets him in. He takes a look around, finally examining the PROFESSOR.

BALLPLAYER So. You got screwed by another shrink.

ACTRESS We were talking.

BALLPLAYER Talking at five in the morning?

PROFESSOR It's hard to believe perhaps.

BALLPLAYER No, it's not hard to believe. If she can talk through the entire world series she can talk until five any morning. Why you got no clothes on?

PROFESSOR It's a dog of a night.

BALLPLAYER Ain't it just.

He takes more gum from his pocket.

BALLPLAYER Get your coat.

He unwraps it.

ACTRESS I'll come when I've finished talking.

He looks at the card.
The card shows a pitcher in action.
He flips the card away. It hits the little toy soldier and knocks him over.

EXT. BROOKLYN STREET. DAY. (1929)
A gang of boys play baseball. One is much taller and older than the rest.
He thwacks a ball and runs around their makeshift diamond, effortlessly scattering the littler boys and sliding home

INT. HOTEL ROOM. NIGHT.
The BALLPLAYER chews a couple of chews.

BALLPLAYER OK. Finish. Talk smart. Tell her what Floyd would have said.

PROFESSOR Floyd?

ACTRESS Freud.

He grins and sits down.

> *BALLPLAYER* She's been to a dozen shrinks. She tells you how she hated her mother and so she can't have stable relationships then you tell her the reason she can't have stable relationships is because she hated her mother!

EXT. STADIUM TUNNEL. DAY.   (1948)
A baseball team, all huge men, run on the spot in a long dark tunnel. Ahead of them is daylight, but it seems miles away.

> *BALLPLAYER (over)* Then she pays you fifty dollars and she comes back next week until you make a pass and she goes and finds another shrink.

INT. HOTEL ROOM. NIGHT.
The BALLPLAYER is sitting, but not relaxed.

> *BALLPLAYER* I seen it all before; me and Floyd, we're old buddies.

> *ACTRESS* Fer-oid!

> *BALLPLAYER* I've met her mother and let me tell you, she's easy to hate. Anyone who hates her mother, there's nothing wrong with them.

> *ACTRESS (quietly)* Stepmother.

> *BALLPLAYER (standing)* I hate you guys, you bunch of...

> *ACTRESS* Honey. Sit down and shut up.

He sits. Takes another pack of gum and pulls out the card.

> *BALLPLAYER* Go ahead. Talk smart.

He glances at the card.

EXT. BROOKLYN STREET. DAY.   (1929)
The tall boy thwacks another ball.
This time it is plucked from the air by his father, who throws it back at him at a tremendous speed; he drops his bat and lifts his arms to defend himself.
The ball whistles past.
The little boys watch frozen in fascination at his lost dignity.

INT. HOTEL ROOM. NIGHT.
The ACTRESS sits down and looks up at the PROFESSOR.

> *ACTRESS* Where were we?

> *PROFESSOR* Mmm?

> *BALLPLAYER* You were discussing her head.

He flips the card at her. It hits her face.

> *ACTRESS* As it happens we were discussing the shape of the physical universe.

> *BALLPLAYER* Easy ones first, huh?

> *ACTRESS* I suppose we could discuss something we all know about but that would limit us to the last nine world series and the names of the seven dwarves.

BALLPLAYER stands, but tired, not threatening.

> *BALLPLAYER* Shift.

> *ACTRESS* Well, six of them at least.

> *BALLPLAYER* One...

EXT. BASEBALL DIAMOND. DAY.
A player slides home. His heel sends up a spray of dirt.

> *ACTRESS (over)* The Shape of the Universe?

INT. HOTEL ROOM. NIGHT.

> *BALLPLAYER* Two...

EXT. BASEBALL DIAMOND. DAY.
Player slides again. An explosion of dirt.

> *PROFESSOR (over)* I think this is not the best time.

INT. HOTEL ROOM. NIGHT.

> *BALLPLAYER* Three...

> *ACTRESS (to Professor)* Please, let's talk. *(to ballplayer)* Try 'four'.

> *BALLPLAYER* Home!

EXT. BASEBALL DIAMOND. DAY.
The player lands bodily, like a war casualty.

> *BALLPLAYER (over)* The man don't want to talk...

INT. HOTEL ROOM. NIGHT.

> ...so get off you butt and come home.

The ACTRESS doesn't move an inch. He contains his frustration and moves back to his chair.

> *ACTRESS* What *is* the Shape of the Universe?

> *PROFESSOR* It's not important. You have things to discuss.

BALLPLAYER Will you tell her the shape of the friggin' universe; I want to get her home.

ACTRESS Please?

PROFESSOR Well...

Standing in the middle of the room with no trousers is hardly conducive, but he does his best, using fingers to demonstrate.

PROFESSOR The Shape of the Universe cannot be described, it can only be imagined. It's really very simple. Imagine a tiny dot. Move the dot and it turns into a line. Move the line and it turns into a circle. Move the circle and it turns into a sphere. Move the sphere and it turns into... the Shape of the Universe.

The ACTRESS attempts the finger patterns.
The BALLPLAYER drums his fingers on his chair.

PROFESSOR You can come closest if you try to imagine turning something absolutely solid inside out, and keep on turning it inside out forever.

ACTRESS Wow.

BALLPLAYER Bullshit. I'll tell you what I think.

He stands and coaches them.

BALLPLAYER I think it's round, like everything else in nature; the sun, the moon, the flowers; are all based on a circle, you know that? Like the world. I don't know what shape you two geniuses think the world is but me and Columbus think it's round, which is a damn lucky thing for the States because if it wasn't for Columbus we'd all be Indians. You ever think of that? Get your coat.

She stays seated.

ACTRESS I'm not coming.

BALLPLAYER Why not?

ACTRESS Because you're an idiot.

BALLPLAYER You want a divorce?

She is rendered speechless. No witty reply.

INT. RESTUARANT. NIGHT.
BALLPLAYER and ACTRESS have finished their meal. She is giggling helplessly. He smiles with strained dignity.
She puts her hands to her mouth. The diamonte watch sparkles.
She slides majestically under the table. He stops smiling and looks acutely embarrassed.

INT. HOTEL ROOM. NIGHT.

BALLPLAYER You want to finish it?

ACTRESS No.

BALLPLAYER Then come home. You come home honey, or I swear I'll go get me a lawyer and I'll disappear so's you can't find me for a change. Bob Dalrymple, he gave me the name of a good man. Look, I wrote it down.

He shows her a crumpled gum packet.

I phoned this man. He said with the reputation you got I'd have no trouble at all. He said it'd be a pleasure.

ACTRESS You phoned a lawyer?

BALLPLAYER You ain't been home for three weeks.

ACTRESS OK.

BALLPLAYER You coming home?

ACTRESS Mmmhmm.

BALLPLAYER OK.

He backs off and gets her coat. She stands, but when the coat is handed out to her, she doesn't slip her arms into it.

ACTRESS Er, I have to use the bathroom first.

She crosses the room slowly. The men watch her. She enters the bathroom.

INT. BATHROOM. NIGHT.
The ACTRESS enters in the dark and switches on the light.
The bathroom has an absurd number of mirrors and is decorated in a dark pink.
She immediately comes face to face with herself, turns and finds herself surrounded by her own image.

INT. BATHROOM. DAY.
The ACTRESS'S fingers slide across a mirrored surface. A smear of blood is left.

INT. SLUM BATHROOM. NIGHT.   (1943)
A smear of bright blue liquid on a dirty mirror.
*The mirror and basin are splattered with blue liquid. A finger
with the nails well chewed makes a pattern in the liquid on the
glass.*

INT. BATHROOM. NIGHT.
The ACTRESS stares at herself, afraid.

INT. SLUM BATHROOM. NIGHT.   (1943)
*The ACTRESS, much younger, stares at herself. She has wet blue
hair and wet blue hands. Blue lines have streaked her face.*

INT. BATHROOM. NIGHT.
*The ACTRESS turns away, closes her eyes, sways, and steadies
herself.*

INT. HOTEL ROOM. NIGHT.
The PROFESSOR has perched on the end of his bed.
*The BALLPLAYER, opening another pack of gum, joins him.
They sit like players on a bench.*

EXT. STADIUM TUNNEL. DAY.
The men run towards the light, but it gets no closer.

INT. HOTEL ROOM. NIGHT.

> *BALLPLAYER* You chew gum?

> *PROFESSOR* No.

BALLPLAYER hands him a piece, which he has to take.

> *PROFESSOR* Thank you.

*BALLPLAYER looks at the card. A player diving backwards for
a catch.*

> *BALLPLAYER* Huh. Who the hell's heard of
> Willy McKormack? You ever heard of Willy
> McKormack? Some kid thinks he's a big shot; they
> put him on a bubble-gum card.

He flips the card away.

> You know haw many bubble-gum series I been in?
> Thirteen. Thirteen series. I been in Chigley's
> Sporting Greats, I been in Pinky's World Series
> Stars 1936, 1937, 1942, 1944, 1945, 1949, and
> 1951. I been in Tip Top Boys' Best Baseball Tips
> showing how best to pitch, swing, deadstop and
> slide, and I been Hubbly Bubbly's Baseball Bites
> best all-rounder nine years running.

*He takes a small pile of cards from his pocket, snaps off the rubber
band, and flips through them for us. All show him, batting or
grinning. Some are identical.*

> *BALLPLAYER* And how many kids you know
> collect? Card for card it must run into millions. I
> must be stuck in albums from here to the Pacific.
> Worldwide. They give gum to little chink kids,

don't they? You liberate them one day, next day
they're making swops. I saw on TV they don't
take beads and junk up the Amazon no more.
They take instant coffee and bubble gum. I could
walk into a little village that's hardly seen a white
man and they'd say, 'Hey, Bighitter; sit down,
have some coffee.'

EXT. BROOKLYN STREET. DAY.
*The BALLPLAYER runs for home base on a makeshift diamond
in the street, but he runs in cod slow motion.*
*A five-year-old Chinese boy throws him out. All the kids he's
playing with cheer themselves ecstatically.*

> *BALLPLAYER (over)* This fame thing's enough to
> give you the heebies, I can tell you. Chigley's,
> Pinky's, Hubbly's and Tip Top.

INT. HOTEL ROOM. NIGHT.
He is pocketing his cards.

> *BALLPLAYER* That's some bubble gum.

> *PROFESSOR* I was on Chewy Fruits' Great
> Scientific Achievements. That's not much though,
> compared to...

> *BALLPLAYER* Thirteen series.

> *PROFESSOR* ...thirteen series.

> *BALLPLAYER* You got a claim though. Some-
> body must have heard of you. (*Shouts*) You OK,
> honey?

INT. BATHROOM. NIGHT.
*The ACTRESS sits applying lipstick to the lips of her mirrored
image.*

> *ACTRESS* I'm OK.

INT. APARTMENT. NIGHT.   (1952)
*A pile of books. We pan down them; Dostoievsky, Chekov,
Stanislavski, Freud, Jung...*

> *BALLPLAYER (over)* Let me tell you something.
> She's smart enough with all that science stuff, but
> it don't mean nothing compared to feelings, you
> know that?

*...the books are piled on top of a TV set. A ballgame is being
shown.*

EXT. BASEBALL TUNNEL. DAY.
The players run towards the light.

INT. HOTEL ROOM. NIGHT.

> *BALLPLAYER* I could kill a man, you know? If
> she ever got it down to one.

He stands and paces, trying to free himself of tension.

BALLPLAYER I get so tightened up, like just before a game, whenever I'm not alone with her, because even the team, my old team, they'd rather stare at her than gab about old times. They treat her like a star or something. Let me tell you; never put a woman up on a pedestal; it makes it too easy for her to kick your teeth down your throat.

The PROFESSOR is almost nodding off in spite of himself.

You know what she needs? She needs a thousand people touching her all of the time and she needs to be alone all of the time also.

EXT. STADIUM TUNNEL. DAY.
The men have nearly reached the light.

BALLPLAYER (over) And I get so tightened up, like I used to just before a game. But now there's no...

The men are about to emerge into the sunlight.

INT. HOTEL ROOM. NIGHT.

BALLPLAYER ...there's no...

He gestures, trying to express himself.

BALLPLAYER It just goes on and on.

He takes a swing with an imaginary baseball bat.

BALLPLAYER Nyah!

Crowds cheer over.
He looks at the PROFESSOR, embarrassed.
The PROFESSOR smiles, stifles a yawn.
The BALLPLAYER crosses to the bathroom door.

BALLPLAYER Honey? You bleeding again?

He gets no reply to his whisper, so moves away.

INT. BATHROOM NIGHT.
The ACTRESS sits disorientated, cooling her face by resting her cheek on an enamelled surface.
She can hear the BALLPLAYER, but far away, talking not to her but of her.

BALLPLAYER (over) She bleeds, you know? She's loose inside. She can't keep a baby in after it gets so big. They keep trying to tighten her up, she keeps getting loose again.

EXT. ORPHANAGE. NIGHT.   (1931)
Child's watch falling through night sky.

BALLPLAYER (over) A baby could kill her, because to keep it they'd have made her so tight it couldn't come out natural, you know?

INT. BATHROOM. NIGHT.
The ACTRESS looks into the mirror.

INT. SLUM BATHROOM. NIGHT.   (1943)
The ACTRESS unwraps a towel from her head and blonde hair falls round her shoulders. Her mouth opens in surprise; she is quite delighted.

INT. BATHROOM. NIGHT.
The ACTRESS smears the lipstick lips on the mirror with her fingers.

BALLPLAYER (over) That's my girl. All bright lights on the outside, but on the inside she fell down from up there and hit the street.

She becomes dizzy, reaches out.

EXT. ORPHANAGE. NIGHT.
The watch falls...

INT. BATHROOM. NIGHT.
The ACTRESS falls...

INT. BASEMENT. NIGHT.
The industrial fan spins faster.

EXT. NEW YORK STREET. NIGHT.
Her white dress flies up.

MAN'S VOICE (over) Five minutes!

A crowd pushes fowards, eating, grinning, talking, and above all, staring.

MAN'S VOICE (over) Five minutes!

A camera flashlight bleaches out the screen.

INT. DORMITORY. NIGHT.   (1931)
A white sheet billows.
Out of it, tossed high in the air, comes the five-year-old child. She screams.

CHILD No!!

INT. CAR. NIGHT.
From the ACTRESS'S point of view, the BALLPLAYER recedes through the rear window of the car.

MAN'S VOICE (over) Five minutes please!

EXT. ORPHANAGE. NIGHT.   (1931)
The watch disappears down the grating.

INT. BATHROOM. NIGHT.
She has almost reached the floor.

MAN'S VOICE (over) Five minutes please!

INT. DRESSING ROOM. DAY.

The ACTRESS, dressed and made up for shooting, but her make-up ruined by the tears on her face holds the telephone in one hand and the diamanté watch in the other. She glances at the watch.

> ACTRESS *(into phone)* Please...!

> MAN'S VOICE *(outside)* Five minutes!

She throws the watch down.

> ACTRESS Please...

> MAN'S VOICE Five minutes, ma'am, if you please!

She slams down the receiver, picks up the whole phone, and slams it down on the watch. The watch shatters.

INT. BATHROOM. NIGHT.
She lands.
Fade.

INT. HOTEL ROOM. NIGHT.
The ACTRESS is unconscious in the PROFESSOR'S bed. The men hover nearby.

> PROFESSOR We should get a doctor.

> BALLPLAYER She'd give us hell.

> PROFESSOR She's ill.

> BALLPLAYER Yeh, she's ill, but she's all right. She always faints in strange bathrooms.

> PROFESSOR I shall have a small word with the night porter, and find another room.

The BALLPLAYER starts to object.

> PROFESSOR No, please. Be my guest.

> BALLPLAYER Did you ask her here?

> PROFESSOR I think she was feeling lonely with all those people.

The PROFESSOR leaves the bedroom area and begins to collect up his scattered calculus. He is watched by the toy soldier. Their gazes meet.

INT. STUDY. DAY.   (1938)
The PROFESSOR and a nine-year-old boy are on the floor playing toy soldiers. The soldiers are arranged with great expertise.
The PROFESSOR manoeuvres a cannon into position and flicks over five soldiers with his finger, very deliberately.

> BOY You can't do that.

> PROFESSOR I did.

> BOY But you mustn't.

> PROFESSOR I have.

INT. HOTEL ROOM. NIGHT.
The BALLPLAYER goes into the bathroom. He looks around and picks up her lipstick off the floor. He makes a half-hearted attempt to wipe the glass clean.
When the glass stays smeared he becomes frustrated and tries harder.
When it still stays smeared he loses his temper. With an imaginary baseball bat he takes swings at the mirrors. Of course, they stay whole.
Energy spent he returns to the bedroom.

INT. HOTEL ROOM. NIGHT.
The BALLPLAYER sits on the edge of the bed and touches the ACTRESS gently.

> ACTRESS Honey?

> BALLPLAYER You did it again.

> ACTRESS I'm OK.

> BALLPLAYER You're a mess.
> I have to say sorry.

> ACTRESS Why?

> BALLPLAYER I went crazy with the bat again. But no damage. Still no damage.

> ACTRESS You know, when I was a girl...

> BALLPLAYER No.

> ACTRESS What?

> BALLPLAYER I don't want to hear. No more stories.

> ACTRESS I'm trying to tell you how it is I love you.

> BALLPLAYER Not a hell of a lot.

> ACTRESS Not how much or how little, how.

> BALLPLAYER How?

> ACTRESS In my way.

> BALLPLAYER What about my way?

> ACTRESS What's that?

> BALLPLAYER My way! My way! What I want.

INT. STUDY. DAY.   (1938)

A brightly coloured child's ball hits a platoon of toy soldiers.

INT. HOTEL ROOM. NIGHT.

The PROFESSOR has gathered his calculus into more or less one pile. He picks up the toy soldier.

INT. STUDY. DAY.   (1938)

The child glowers at the old man then picks up the brightly coloured ball and throws it at the PROFESSOR's soldiers.
It knocks over a couple of dozen men, bounces up and hits the PROFESSOR on the head.

INT. HOTEL ROOM. NIGHT.

The PROFESSOR puts down the soldier carefully and tries to pick up the calculus, but it's too heavy. He makes a hands-down gesture and leaves it.
He picks up his shoes and carries them out of the suite, closing the door behind him gently.
The BALLPLAYER has crawled onto the bed.

> *ACTRESS* Do you still want a child?

> *BALLPLAYER* I want the one we already had.

> *ACTRESS* I was under contract. What if I was careful?

> *BALLPLAYER* I don't care no more.

> *ACTRESS* It might be a son.

> *BALLPLAYER* And it might be a fucking mess.

> *ACTRESS* I want to be pregnant.

He curls up, his head in her lap.

> *BALLPLAYER* It'd never get born.

> *ACTRESS* This one will.

> *BALLPLAYER* You're broken, you're bruised, and I don't know how to love you any more.

> *ACTRESS* Shh...

She strokes his head. He closes his eyes.

> *ACTRESS* I want, please God if it happens...a daughter! No! A son.

Her face full of a strange excitement.

> *ACTRESS* Honey. I think I am. Honey?

He is asleep. She closes her eyes. Reaches up and turns off the light. It is almost morning.

INT. ELEVATOR. DAWN.

Travelling down, the INDIAN looks across at his passenger's feet. It is the PROFESSOR. They are bare. The INDIAN smiles.

EXT. NEW YORK STREET. DAWN.

The red neon light, flashing uselessly now, switches itself off.

INT. HOTEL ROOM. DAWN.

Both sleeping.

INT. HOTEL FOYER. DAWN.

The PROFESSOR, curled up in a corner seat, half hidden by enormous pot plants.

EXT. NEW YORK. DAWN.

High above the streets. The sun is not quite up yet, but there is birdsong and traffic noise beginning.

EXT. PACIFIC ISLAND. DUSK.   (1944)

An overweight soldier advances through jungle growth. He moves painfully cautiously, his ears and eyes at their most alert.
The birdsong and traffic are heard over.

EXT. NEW YORK STREET. DAWN.

A few early birds take to the streets.

EXT. PACIFIC ISLAND. DUSK.   (1944)

The soldier still advances. Suddenly, from lower than expected, a Japanese face appears. The soldier, startled, shoots wildly.

INT. SENATOR'S BATHROOM. DAWN.

The PROSTITUTE, reaching for her make-up bag, knocks a whisky bottle and glass over into the sink.

EXT. PACIFIC ISLAND. DUSK.

The soldier shoots in fear six times. Only the third shot hits the Japanese man, but kills him.
There is an unbearable silence. The soldier has blown his cover. He has to continue his journey through the tangled undergrowth in even greater danger than before.

INT. SENATOR'S ROOM. DAWN.

The SENATOR wakes suddenly, sweating.
He can hear noises from the bathroom. The PROSTITUTE singing to herself. He sits up and watches her through the open door. She stops singing.
She unclips and removes her blonde Monroe wig; underneath she's a brunette. She wipes make-up from her face.
Fade.

INT. HOTEL FOYER. DAY.

The PROFESSOR still snoozes behind the plant.
The hotel is busier now. The INDIAN passes the desk with a cup of coffee. The NIGHT MAN is changing over to the DAY MAN.

> *NIGHT MAN* Don't he ever sleep?

EXT./INT. ELEVATOR. DAY.

The INDIAN gets into his elevator and closes the gate. The elevator rises.

INT. ELEVATOR. DAY.

The INDIAN watches groups or pairs or individuals waiting for the elevator as it passes them. He smiles politely at them and sips his coffee but never stops. Each time he passes:

INDIAN Going up.

EXT. ROOF. DAY.

The INDIAN steps out onto the hotel roof and surveys the city below and above. He finishes his coffee and places the cup next to a dozen or so cups arranged along the parapet of the building. He breathes deeply and goes into a traditional greeting of the day. When finished, he returns to the elevator.

INT. ELEVATOR. DAY.

The elevator stops descending and he opens the gates. The SENATOR enters the car. He stands as far away from the INDIAN as possible. The lift descends a couple of floors.
The INDIAN opens the gates and the BALLPLAYER enters, looking surprisingly spruce under the circumstances. He is followed by another white man, a black man and a JAPANESE DELEGATE wearing a peace conference lapel badge.
The SENATOR pulls himself up attempting and just succeeding to avoid body contact with anyone.

INT. HOTEL ROOM. DAY.

The ACTRESS is alone, asleep. The connecting doors are open. The room is light and white and airy.

INT. ELEVATOR. DAY.

The elevator arrives at the next floor down. Two more JAPANESE are waiting. As the INDIAN opens the gates they call to their colleagues down the corridor, who enter the elevator after them.
All in all about a dozen men crowd into the elevator, crushing the SENATOR to the rear. He looks extremely uncomfortable as the gates are closed.
One floor down two RUSSIANS enter the elevator crushing the SENATOR even more between two JAPANESE men. Sweat breaks out on his forehead and one can sense his dire claustrophobia.

EXT. HIROSHIMA. DAY.   (1945)

The JAPANESE WOMAN washes her hand in the river.

INT. ELEVATOR. DAY.

The SENATOR is in obvious distress. One expects him to yell out any minute. He tries to get a hand into his pocket but his arm is trapped.
The elevator stops again.

SENATOR Full! We're full up!

But it is the ground floor. Everyone leaves the car. The SENATOR cannot move for a moment. He mops his brow. The INDIAN smiles at him.

INT. HOTEL FOYER. DAY.

The BALLPLAYER strides out of the hotel past two men in black waiting by the desk.
One turns to look as he passes.

FIRST CIA MAN See him?

SECOND CIA MAN Who?

FIRST CIA MAN Whatsisname.

The SENATOR beckons to them and they join him. He leads them past the elevator and they take the stairs.
The PROFESSOR still sleeps behind the greenery.

INT. HOTEL ROOM. DAY.

The ACTRESS still sleeps. She's surrounded by a businesslike knocking on the door. The light hurts her eyes so she buries her head beneath the sheets.

INT. CORRIDOR. DAY.

The SENATOR is completely out of breath. All three men breathe heavily. When they get no answer he opens the door and goes in.

INT. HOTEL ROOM. DAY.

SENATOR Professor? Professor?

He enters followed by the men and crosses to the connecting door.

SENATOR Sorry to wake you Professor but I have here a warrant issued by the Department of Defence authorizing me to search your room and belongings for any material or artifact that might be deemed harmful to the security of the United States of America. That OK by you?

He waggles his warrant and grins charmingly.
The ACTRESS emerges from the sheets, frowning.
The SENATOR is astonished, then disorientated, then grins.

SENATOR Now that is quite astonishing. You could be the splitting image...

ACTRESS I know. If I was eight years younger and took more care.

SENATOR Right.

She finds her dark glasses on the bedside table and puts them on.

SENATOR Er... this is room 1614? The Professor's room.

ACTRESS He took another. I don't know where.

SENATOR Well wherever he is he ought to be ashamed of himself. (*To the men*) Go find him.

The MEN leave.

SENATOR Do you mind if I wait?

ACTRESS Not if you don't mind my throwing up.

SENATOR You've taken a dislike to me I can tell. It's my fault for bursting in on you like this. You know, you two could be sisters. Must be kind of advantageous for a girl like you.

ACTRESS What do you want?

SENATOR touches her hair.

SENATOR That's the real thing, ain't it?

ACTRESS What do you want?

SENATOR Just a bunch of stuff that was hanging around here.

He looks around the room and lights on the calculus.

ACTRESS Who are you?

SENATOR Oh, I'm just an all-American boy ten years on and ten years weary. I shouldn't think he was much of a customer, was he?

ACTRESS Are you for real?

SENATOR (*Turns back to her*) You think I'm not?

ACTRESS I think you're fat.

SENATOR You're very charming.

ACTRESS You're very fat.

EXT. HILLSIDE. DAY.   (1920)

A fat boy with a pack on his back is climbing to the top of a hill with great difficulty. Other boys who have been to the top already whoop past him on their race back downhill.
He looks back at them, looks up at the top, almost gives up, but decides to plod on.

INT. HOTEL ROOM. DAY.

The SENATOR walks slowly back to the bed, gets horribly close to her.

SENATOR You want me to call the vice squad?

ACTRESS No.

SENATOR Then shut the fuck up.

He turns and walks back to the calculus, which he kneels down to.

ACTRESS Don't touch that. What are you doing?

SENATOR (*Tidying the pile*) My job. This here's a warrant authorizing me to confiscate any suspicionable material under the State Protection Act of 1912. Your client of last night may not be all he seems.

ACTRESS He's a genius.

SENATOR Doesn't bother me. I have no sense of decency.

ACTRESS He has the respect of half the world.

SENATOR I have authorization.

He picks up the calculus and puts it on the television set. The ACTRESS sits up, wrapping the sheet around her.

ACTRESS Is this some sort of um... Is this politics?

SENATOR looks at her sharply.

SENATOR You know, one thing I've learned about Communists is they think everything's politics. You give them a parking ticket and they think it's politics. You know the best way to catch a Communist? You give them three parking tickets in a row and if they start picking up the phone listening for taps you know you got one.

ACTRESS How do you know if they pick up the phone?

SENATOR You tap it. They ain't paranoid, they's Communist.

He picks up the calculus and turns to go.

ACTRESS Now hold on!

She clambers across the bed at great risk to her modesty.

ACTRESS Where are you going? Where are you taking that? There are no copies, will it be safe? Are you acting officially?

SENATOR Well good grief if I wasn't there'd be nothing to stop me destroying the stuff altogether.

ACTRESS Is that what you're going to do?

SENATOR That's none of your damn business! My orders are to find this stuff and sit on it. Then I get a call and I hand it back or I burn the goddam thing.

ACTRESS No! I'll report you!

She rushes across and picks up the phone. The SENATOR cannot help but steal glances at her body as it flashes out of the sheet.

SENATOR Who to?

ACTRESS The FBI. CIA. I don't care, NBC. What's to stop me?

SENATOR Common sense I should think. A little adverse publicity might not do a girl like you any harm, but think of the Professor's position.

She puts the phone down. He makes for the door, but she puts herself between him and it.

ACTRESS No! Please. At least wait until he's back. You don't understand; his work's priceless.

SENATOR I'm not playing games here. My concern happens to be the survival of the free world.

She touches the calculus, would like to take it from him.

ACTRESS Do you realize what this is? It isn't just the culmination of a man's life work, although Lord knows... It's a set of calculations that come close to describing the shape of Space-Time. If you'd just let him finish, he'll have calculated how it all fits. How everything is.

EXT. HILLSIDE. DAY.   (1920)
The fat boy sits alone on the top of the hill. It is dusk and almost silent. He surveys the world.
The few people he can see are little nothings.

INT. HOTEL ROOM. DAY.

SENATOR You ain't talking to green-corn you know. I've given some thought as to the importance of those documents and I have come to the conclusion that the shape of Space-Time is of fuck all importance to any of us.

EXT. HILLSIDE. DAY.   (1920)
The boy throws a stick or stone out in the vague hope it might hit someone far below.

INT. HOTEL ROOM. DAY.

SENATOR It's just paper.

ACTRESS Well he wouldn't agree and neither do I. Please? Leave it? For me?

SENATOR You know, it's uncanny. At times you er... you've really studied the lady haven't you?

She breaks away, tightening her sheet. Then turns.

ACTRESS I could let you have money.

SENATOR (laughs) You trying to bribe a United States Government Official?

ACTRESS Yes.

SENATOR Takes a lot of dollars to buy a man.

Where'd a girl like you get money like that?

ACTRESS I'm not a girl.

SENATOR I was being polite.

He crosses back to the TV and puts the calculus down again. In fact, he moves to put the ACTRESS between him and the windows, rendering the sheet less opaque. She is aware of this, and can't help enjoying it.

SENATOR Well, you've tried appealing to my back pocket and to my intelligence. Are there any more little persuasions you'd like to try?

She laughs. It had to come.

INT. AUDITION ROOM. DAY.   (1945)
The girls file out past one of the fat men, who holds open the door and closes it after them.
Only the ACTRESS remains with the men. The men smile.

ACTRESS (over) Maybe.

INT. HOTEL ROOM. DAY.

SENATOR I beg your pardon, what was that?

She goes blank for a moment, looks over at the calculus.

ACTRESS All right.

SENATOR Do I understand you correctly? In return for my leaving the calculus you're offering me sexual favours?

ACTRESS A sexual favour.

She seems to oscillate now between tremendous self-confidence and a complete lack of it, between her image and her state of mind.

ACTRESS I mean, what the hell? After all, it's not me you want, it it? It's her.

She takes hold of his necktie and leads him to the bed. He watches her suspiciously, begins to sweat.
She clambers onto the bed. He stands beside it.
She undoes the buttons of his pants.

INT. SENATOR'S ROOM. NIGHT.
The SENATOR on his back. The PROSTITUTE works on him.
She looks at her watch briefly. He sees her do it.

INT. HOTEL ROOM. DAY.
The ACTRESS undoes another button.
He slaps her face, this opens her body to him.
He hits her with his fist in the belly. She doubles up and rolls back onto the bed.

SENATOR I ain't ever paid for it in my life; least of all with my integrity!

She groans. He is unsure of what to do.

SENATOR Did I hurt you?

He suddenly finds it very hot. He goes to the window and throws it open. He sees the billboard, the dead neon. (No names.)

SENATOR My son had her picture on his wall! I whipped his ass! They call her a goddam Goddess. I mean shit, she's mortal ain't she? I mean she only got where she is the same way as you.

He sits cautiously on the end of the bed, anger turns to worry. She remains curled up.

SENATOR Listen, a girl like you gotta look after her little body. Your little body ain't worth no pile of paper. If I hurt you I apologize. Nothing personal.

There's a polite knock on the door. The SENATOR starts. He leaves the bed and closes the separating doors.
The PROFESSOR comes in cautiously. Is shocked to see the SENATOR.

PROFESSOR Good morning.

SENATOR Good morning.

The PROFESSOR moves towards the bedroom.

SENATOR The lady's getting dressed. Are you willing to testify?

PROFESSOR No.

SENATOR All we're asking for is a few wise words.

PROFESSOR The few I have I shall address to the peace conference.

SENATOR I have a better idea. We need your support. We do need it.

PROFESSOR Why? Why now?

SENATOR The Atomic Energy Commission comes under review next month. Another few bright young Congressmen are going to try to put the lid on the Nevada tests, in spite of the fact that we have to match the Soviet initiative! President needs to be backed by top men. You're the top man.

PROFESSOR No!

INT. BEDROOM AREA. DAY.
The ACTRESS writhes.

PROFESSOR (over) Teller! Oppenheimer!

SENATOR (over) No use politically.

INT. LIVING AREA. DAY.

SENATOR Oppenheimer's name casts a shadow of doom since Nagasaki.

The word has an effect on the PROFESSOR. He takes out his watch and fingers it.

SENATOR Besides, the world chooses it's own heroes. There's no shadow on the pristine world of theory...

The watch nervously toyed with.

SENATOR No strains of Armageddon in $E=Mc^2$, even if Mc^2 does equal one fuck of a big bang.

The watch flips open.

INT. BEDROOM AREA. DAY.
The ACTRESS doubles up in intense pain, almost falling off the bed.

INT. LIVING AREA. DAY.
The watch reads 8.15.
The SENATOR moves across and stands over the calculus.

SENATOR I can tell you're a man who likes things clear and simple, well here it is clear and simple. You say one wrong thing at the conference or the hearings or any damn public place and I shall personally see to it that this here 'life's work' goes up in smoke.

INT. BEDROOM. DAY.
The ACTRESS'S hand grips the sheet tight. A nail snaps.

INT. LIVING AREA. DAY.
The PROFESSOR's face. Miles away.

SENATOR See, there comes a time in every man's life when he has to figure out what's more important; what he thinks, or what he does.

The PROFESSOR moves across and puts his hand on the calculus, then picks it up and takes it to the open window. Then he throws it out.

EXT. NEW YORK. DAY.
High above the street the sheets of calculus explode and fall.

INT. BEDROOM AREA. DAY.
Some sheets of calculus blow past the bedroom window, a couple are pasted briefly outside the pane.

ACTRESS No..! Oh God, no.

But she hasn't seen them. She struggles to sit up, then swings her legs over the side of the bed.

INT. LIVING AREA. DAY.
SENATOR You crazy son of a bitch. That's your

only copy. You lost your work.

PROFESSOR Mmm.

He looks around.

PROFESSOR And I have lost my shoes.

INT. BEDROOM AREA. DAY.
The ACTRESS feels beneath the sheets; her hand comes out covered in blood. She moves over; there is more blood on the sheets. She has miscarried.

EXT. NEW YORK STREET. DAY.
Calculus falls.

INT. BEDROOM AREA. DAY.
The ACTRESS takes a handful of tissues from the bedside table and puts them into herself.

EXT. NEW YORK STREET. DAY.
Calculus lands and gets trampled by uninterested feet.

INT. BEDROOM AREA. DAY.
She gets up from the bed very unsteadily, covers up the mess instinctively, and goes into the bathroom.

INT. BATHROOM. DAY.
She stumbles.
The ACTRESS's fingers slide across a mirrored surface.
A smear of blood is left.

INT. HOTEL CORRIDOR. DAY.
The BALLPLAYER, with coffee and a bag of doughnuts, is returning to the room.
The SENATOR comes out of it. They almost collide.

BALLPLAYER I don't believe it. Every time I turn my back there's a different man in my wife's room.

SENATOR Do I know you from someplace?

BALLPLAYER Yes you do, now who are you?

SENATOR I just had some business with the Professor.

BALLPLAYER You did huh? Come in and sit down.

The BALLPLAYER seems as wide as the corridor.

SENATOR I'm in a hurry.

BALLPLAYER Listen, until I've spoken to my wife your choice is to come inside and sit down unaided, or lie down out here with assistance.

SENATOR Are you threatening me?

BALLPLAYER No, I never had to hit an

intelligent man.

The PROFESSOR comes out on the trail of his shoes.

BALLPLAYER *(To Senator)* Get your butt inside.

SENATOR Could you talk some sense into this man?

PROFESSOR I'm told it's not possible.

He heads for the elevator.

SENATOR Listen, we're all civilized human beings here...

PROFESSOR His business was with me. Please, let him go.

The BALLPLAYER lets him go, and the SENATOR follows the PROFESSOR down the hall. The PROFESSOR enters the elevator.

INT. ELEVATOR. DAY.
The INDIAN smiles as the PROFESSOR enters, and closes the gates immediately. The SENATOR is left outside as the elevator descends.

INT. CORRIDOR. DAY.
The SENATOR, stranded, is being watched by the BALLPLAYER. He decides to take the stairs.
The BALLPLAYER goes in.

INT. HOTEL ROOM. DAY.
He looks around for her, and hears a sound from the bathroom. He goes to the door.

BALLPLAYER Honey?

ACTRESS *(off)* Mmmm?

BALLPLAYER It's OK. Take your time.

He sits on a chair next to the door, pulling it close. He's obviously used to conversations like this.

BALLPLAYER I got it all figured out. I had a long walk. I had a think. You want a kid, I want a kid. We get on most of the time but the problem is most of the time you can't stand me, right? And why can't you stand me? Because you think I'm stupid. Well let me reveal to you a secret; I am not stupid. I just enjoy appearing to be stupid. From an early age I have revelled in the appearance of stupidity, which has given me a great deal of time to think. So I've been thinking, and what I've decided is that if you still want me to smarten up, well I figure you're worth it.

INT. BATHROOM. DAY.
She is slowly putting herself together. She washes blood from her hands.

BALLPLAYER (over) So what I figure is while you finish your movies I'll sit down and read a few good books. You can quiz me.

INT. HOTEL ROOM. DAY.

BALLPLAYER And I'll get rid of the TV so there's no more TV and no more TV dinners. If you like, no more ballgames. You come home. I'll smarten up. We'll have a couple of kids.

He is chewing. He takes his gum out of his mouth.

BALLPLAYER No more gum.

Sticks it under the chair.

ACTRESS (off) Um... honey?

He comes closer to the door.

BALLPLAYER Yes?

INT. BATHROOM. DAY.

ACTRESS It's over.

INT. HOTEL ROOM. DAY.

BALLPLAYER You think so?

ACTRESS (over) Yeh, you'd better call up your lawyer freind.

A pause as he takes this in.

BALLPLAYER Yeh, I think so too.

He takes out a pack of gum.

BALLPLAYER Maybe I'm that smart.

He walks away into the other part of the room. Before finishing unwrapping the gum he turns suddenly, walks back, and opens the bathroom door.

INT. BATHROOM. DAY.

She is sitting on the lavatory. She pulls the sheet up to her neck and sits there like a frightened animal. No blood is visible.
His impulse to go to her is conquered by his instinct to keep his distance.
They simply don't know where to go from here.

BALLPLAYER You want some advice? You've got to figure out what you want.

ACTRESS Well...

She is in tears, but stops him coming to her.

ACTRESS I don't want you.

BALLPLAYER What do you want?

ACTRESS I don't want to want.

BALLPLAYER Yeh, but what do you want?

ACTRESS I want to go, do you understand, I want to go!

She buries her head in her lap.
He is at a loss, so looks at her a long time, then leaves.

INT. ELEVATOR. DAY.
The INDIAN opens the gates. The PROFESSOR enters with his shoes in his hands, and smiles. The INDIAN closes the gates. As the elevator moves, he turns to the PROFESSOR.

INDIAN I know you. You are Cherokee.

PROFESSOR I'm an old fool. You are Cherokee.

INDIAN No, I am lift attendant now. I get paycheck, I eat hotdog. I go up and down.

PROFESSOR I met one of your people once. It was at Harvard Observatory. In the driveway. He was collecting garbage. He told me that all true Cherokee believe wherever they are, there is the centre of the Universe. Is that so?

INDIAN (nods) But is hard to believe in elevator. I go up and down. I watch TV. I no longer Cherokee. But I watch TV. I see your face, I hear your thoughts, and so I know; you are Cherokee.

PROFESSOR I don't want to be at the centre of anything, least of all...

INDIAN But there are thoughts in your head, will lead you there.

The PROFESSOR'S eyes become dark.

EXT. HIROSHIMA. DAY.   (1945)
The burning hand.

INT. CORRIDOR. DAY.
The elevator stops, the INDIAN opens the gates.
The BALLPLAYER waits, opening a pack of gum.
He puts the gum in his mouth and looks at the card.
As he and the PROFESSOR pass each other he hands him the card.
It's the BALLPLAYER's picture.

BALLPLAYER Every five or six packs.

PROFESSOR Thank you.

He watches as the BALLPLAYER gets in and begins to descend. When he's gone, he puts the card into his pocket.

INT. BATHROOM. DAY.

The ACTRESS applies lipstick. She is dressed, except for shoes. She teases her hair, pulls herself together as best she can.

INT. HOTEL ROOM. DAY.

The PROFESSOR comes in. The ACTRESS comes out of the bathroom.
She pulls a counterpane over the bed, and checks that there is no sign of violence, then joins him in the living area.

PROFESSOR Hello.

ACTRESS Hi. Um, there was a man.

PROFESSOR I know.

ACTRESS Did he take your work? I think he took your work.

PROFESSOR I know. He didn't.

ACTRESS Thank God.

PROFESSOR I threw it out of the window.

ACTRESS What? You're joking.

PROFESSOR No. It was fun.

ACTRESS You're serious. You threw it away?

PROFESSOR Yes

ACTRESS The only copy.

PROFESSOR The fifth.

ACTRESS What? I don't understand.

PROFESSOR It was the fifth copy.

ACTRESS You mean you have copies! Oh God.

PROFESSOR No, I have no copies. I have destroyed four copies. Five copies.

ACTRESS I'm sorry, I'm not following you.

He packs his things into his gladstone.

PROFESSOR I have finished my work four times. Each time I've... burned the calculus and started over. I remember a little more this time than last but there is so much mechanical mathematics I forget most of what I did before. So I do the work and then I burn the work. Four times now.

He closes the bag. Sits to put on his shoes.

ACTRESS But if you've finished... If you studied it you'd know how it all fits, how it all works; you'd know everything.

PROFESSOR I am seventy years old. I wouldn't survive the publicity. I want to die quietly where I can just slip off the edge of this painful world. Like Columbus never did. Unfortunately. What was it your husband said? If Columbus had slipped up we'd all still be Indians. Cherokee. Instead, what are we? Americans.

He goes to the window and looks out.

And listen to us. He is the most knowledgeable, I am this much knowledgeable.

The ACTRESS, listening.

She is the most beautiful, I am this much beautiful.

EXT. NEW YORK STREET. DAY.

The street below, pedestrians milling. The SENATOR among them.

PROFESSOR *(over)* He is the most powerful. I am hardly powerful at all.

The SENATOR is jostled as he tries to cross the road in the throng.

PROFESSOR *(over)* They will not take responsibility for their world!

The BALLPLAYER is stopped for an autograph. He signs.

PROFESSOR *(over)* They want to load it onto the shoulders of a few.

INT. HOTEL ROOM. DAY.

PROFESSOR And the weight of so many people's worlds, I tell you, it's... [too heavy]

She loses her temper suddenly and confronts him.

ACTRESS Look, would you stop talking so goddam smart! I've heard enough! It just sounds like words. I've heard enough words.

She calms herself.

I came here to know you and all you've done is hide behind words. Now what are you hiding from?

He looks her way sharply.

PROFESSOR Nothing.

ACTRESS Don't lie to me.

PROFESSOR (moving past her) Listen...

ACTRESS What are you afraid of?

PROFESSOR Nothing.

ACTRESS Liar! What are you afraid of?

He sits on the bed.

INT. STUDY. DAY.   (1945)
The PROFESSOR stands listening to a wireless on the mantlepiece beside him. His watch is also there; he picks it up.

WIRELESS ...following announcement from the War Office...

INT. HOTEL ROOM. DAY.
The ACTRESS joins him on the bed.

ACTRESS Tell me.

A pause. She adjusts the sheet unobtrusively, as a patch of blood was showing.

INT. HOSPITAL. DAY.   (1945)
A sheet pulled up over a burned face we hardly see.

INT. HOTEL ROOM. DAY.

PROFESSOR There's something...

ACTRESS What?

PROFESSOR A thought.

ACTRESS Tell me.

PROFESSOR No.

ACTRESS Please.

INT. STUDY. DAY.   (1945)
PROFESSOR still listens.

WIRELESS ...official observers report the explosion took place at 7.15 p.m. today, or at 8.15 a.m. Japanese time.

He opens his watch. It says 8.15.

INT. BEDROOM. DAY.

PROFESSOR (whispers) We burned children.

It takes her some time to take this in. She has to stand and move away. Then turns.

ACTRESS No. You're not responsible for that. You don't believe you're responsible. Not for that.

She crouches in front of him. Takes his hand.

ACTRESS Tell me the truth.

PROFESSOR (looks at her) There's something worse.

ACTRESS What could be worse?

PROFESSOR I don't know!! And I must not think about it.

She moves away, lost for words.
She finds her shoes accidentally. Puts them on.
In the bright sunlight, she casts a sharp shadow across the floor.
The PROFESSOR watches her shadow.

EXT. HIROSHIMA. DAY.   (1945)
There are shadows on the ground that do not move. They once were people.

INT. BEDROOM. DAY.
The ACTRESS finishes with her shoes and tries to think of something to say.

ACTRESS Umm... I have to go.

She finds her coat and picks it up. Underneath it is her shooting script.

ACTRESS Do you want to hear my lines?

She opens the script, eager to snap the PROFESSOR out of his grim reverie. She reads, becoming unbearably cute and mannered, à la Monroe.

ACTRESS I, er, take a pot-roast from the oven, I hear the doorbell, I run across the apartment removing my apron, I kiss the man...

She turns a page.

... I disappear.

She shrugs, embarrassed.

ACTRESS No words.
He looks up at her, immensely sad.

ACTRESS Look, it's over! They won't use those things again. They've said they never will.

PROFESSOR They always have.

ACTRESS No. It's different now. I mean, figure it out; all those with their fingers on the button are the same people who own the stuff that would get blown to blazes, so they'll never do it. Unless of course they could blow up all the people and leave the buildings standing, which they can't.

The PROFESSOR'S face freezes.
The ACTRESS feels a sudden little pain in her belly.
The PROFESSOR closes his eyes, tight shut.
There is an enormous explosion.
The window implodes and an intense white light fills the room.
A wild hot wind races around the room. It lifts her skirt.
She tries desperately to keep it down.
The PROFESSOR watches, his hair wild.

EXT. NEW YORK. DAY.
Sheets of wind-blown calculus lodge themselves in little corners of the city; a hot dog stall, a cinema booth, obviously American corners.

EXT. HIROSHIMA. DAY. (1945)
Other sheets of calculus lodge themselves in a Japanese garden, or the entrance to a tea house.

INT. HOTEL ROOM. DAY.
The room begins to fly apart.
Then combustion. Parts of the room ignite.

EXT. NEW YORK AND HIROSHIMA. DAY.
The pages of calculus spontaneously combust.

INT. HOTEL ROOM. DAY.
The ACTRESS'S dress spontaneously combusts.
She struggles to put it out; her hair catches light.
She burns.
He watches.

EXT. HIROSHIMA. DAY. (1945)
A woman's hair hangs from the door of a wrecked streetcar. The rest of her is buried.
Shadows that were people. Fires still burn nearby.

INT. HOTEL ROOM. DAY.
The ACTRESS, charred and crumbling, falls.
He watches.

EXT. HIROSHIMA. DAY. (1945)
A distorted hand with shortened fingers reaches upwards to the sky. It's fingers burn with blue flames. A dark blue liquid runs from the hand to the ground.
A Japanese woman lies blackened in the road by a river.
Her hand burns.
Nearby a clock burns. It has stopped at 8.15.

INT. HOTEL ROOM. DAY.
The room once more in perfect order.
The ACTRESS, pristine, puts on her dark glasses and opens the door.
  ACTRESS Bye.

END.

Nicolas Roeg compares notes with Gil Evans.

AFTERWORD

The cinema seems at its most compelling when it deals with myths, either when it is creating its own or when it draws on those already established. Perhaps this is because it is able, more than any other medium, to give them a sense of reality... We are there. We see it happen.

I believe reality surpasses our imagination and in a film we see breathing and moving before our eyes, things we never saw even in our dreams. We know they are real because somewhere in our subconscious we still believe the first of all the myths of cinema...'The camera cannot lie'.

I read somewhere. I think it was Eric Bentley in *The Life of the Drama* that melodrama depends for its power on the degree of fear it can arouse and farce on the degree of aggression.

I hope that 'Insignificance' is a Real, Mythical, Melodramic Farce.

Nicolas Roeg

'...the same old myths that made
The early 'stage successes'
Still 'hold the boards' and still are played,
With new effects and dresses...'

Henry Austin Dobson
'The Drama of the Doctor's Window'

The Faery Queen, even myths have wings.

ACKNOWLEDGEMENTS

Notes

1   Quartet Books, London, 1978.   2   *The Crucial Decade – And After: America, 1945-1960* (Vintage Books, Random House, New York 1983).   3   Arthur Barker, London, 1954.   4   Schocken, New York, 1960.   5   *Mandate for Change 1953-1956: The White House Years* (Heinemann 1963).   6   Sun Chief, university - educated Hopi Indian, in his autobiography.   7   *Touch the Earth*, (Penguin).   8   In the Smithsonian Institution, Washington, DC.   9   Shorter Oxford English Dictionary.